HANDWRITING

Peter West

Handwriting

SAFFRON WALDEN
THE C.W. DANIEL COMPANY LIMITED

First published in 1986 in the United Kingdom by
Allison & Busby Limited, London
Revised and republished in 2003 by
The C.W. Daniel Company Limited,
1 Church Path, Saffron Walden,
CB10 1JP, United Kingdom

© Pentagon 1986 & 2003

ISBN 0 85207 364 X

The author has asserted his rights under the Copyright Design
and Patent Act 1988 (and under any comparable provision of
any comparable law in any jurisdiction whatsoever) to be
identified as the author of this work.

After all this time it is not possible to find all, if any,
of the authors who have contributed examples of their
handwriting and or signature used within these pages.
Where certain graphological points have been illustrated
within a sample it has been with that intention only
in mind: personal criticism of an individual has
not been intended.

Production in association with
Book Production Consultants plc,
25–27 High Street, Chesterton, Cambridge, CB4 1ND.
Printed in Great Britain by
St Edmundsbury Press Ltd, Bury St Edmunds, Suffolk

Contents

Before reading further, write a short note to someone you know reasonably well.

Make it at least 75–100 words in length on a sheet of A4 unlined paper. Don't worry too much about content and try to write in your usual style, but when you sign it, date it as well. Put it in an envelope and put the envelope somewhere safe until you have read this book.

This is probably your last chance to write with an unprejudiced hand.

Introduction

Handwriting is a most personal method of communicating, particularly when emphasized with a signature. Society and the law recognize this as being a unique and unmistakable form of identification: to forge either can incur severe punishment in most civilized countries.

In acknowledging this feature of handwriting we are also saying that it reflects character and personality. Note how easily we recognize the styles of friends and relatives just by looking at the envelope when we receive our post. We extend this exercise to assess the script of strangers and, by following set procedures laid down by years of experience and study, we can arrive at certain conclusions regarding their character and personality. This suggests a scientific basis for analysis. However, there is also an art to interpreting character from handwriting using these rules. Thus graphology, like astrology or chirology, may be termed an art-science.

One cannot use it to foretell the future, although a graphologist may be able to accurately assess the reactions of a particular writer if and when certain conditions arise. One cannot use it to identify the sex or the age of a writer, nor tell if he or she is left-handed. There may be tell-tale signs of extreme youth or old age, but few left-handed writers can be detected.

Basically, handwriting reflects the mood and thinking of the individual at the time of writing. Therefore, writing may vary slightly according to how the writer feels — and this will have a bearing on the formation of the script.

Of course, much may depend on to whom and for what purpose the handwriting is being executed: a letter to a friend, a request for some information, a message giving information, a love letter or a job application. A graphologist will rarely be concerned with the subject matter, for it may be misleading. Every part of the sample should come under scrutiny.

Ideally, a sample will be at least 75–100 words in length, on unlined paper at least A4 size. It should wherever possible include a signature. The writer should use a ball point or fountain pen, not

7

a pencil or a fibre-tip pen, and should not copy from a book or magazine. The sample should be in prose form, not poetry, and it is preferable to use one that has been written naturally, such as a recent letter, and not one that has been written specifically for the purpose of analysis.

The best place to start is at the end and then work back towards the beginning. This may sound like strange advice, but it isn't. Most writers, whatever their subject or reason for writing, tend to be self-conscious at the beginning but become less so as the work proceeds. Once you become involved with your message, you become less involved with the construction of the actual script. The result is that the end of the majority of samples is likely to be more naturally executed than the beginning.

It is important to remember that each sign, trait or clue must be treated as such. An occasional sign may mean just that. You must also remember that all facets of personality have positive and negative aspects.

Observe and evaluate the whole sample, never just a part; learn to balance and counterbalance. Take up a pen and trace a line or word for yourself. See how the original was created.

Handwriting assessment is a logical process. Tidy writing may indicate a tidy mind, but it may also show a tendency to timidity. Hopeless scrawls do not always refer to poor education; it may be that the mind operates so swiftly the hand simply cannot keep up, the result being an illegible mess. By tracing a word here and there you will begin to understand your subject more fully — a picture of the personality will begin to build up as you progress.

A signature represents the "outer image" that the writer wishes to present to the outside world. Often, people will use two different signatures, one for formal or business correspondence, the other for more private, personal matters. Caution, therefore, should be exercised when looking at a single example, particularly when you don't have any other writing from the same source.

The main body of the text will provide information on the physical, mental and emotional state at the time of writing — the "inner man" or woman — and the signature will reflect the outer image. Later, we shall see how to detect conflict, if any, between the two.

The finer details of analysis require division of the component parts of the script; slant, zones, size, loops (or lack of them), "connectedness", style, form level, capitals, margins, legibility, speed, and punctuation. Handwriting may appear thick or thin, be spaced widely or in narrow form. There may be little flourishes at the beginning or end of words or letters, which, to the untrained eye, mean little. Even the colour of the ink and the way numbers are formed tell their part. An envelope will give interesting clues as well.

Some experts suggest that there is inevitably some form of control in the way an envelope is addressed: it is not so spontaneous as the letter it contains. Nevertheless, comparison between the writing on the envelope and the message inside can often be very revealing.

Handwriting is a silent and expressive gesture that none of us can afford to ignore. People study handwriting for a variety of reasons.

There are specially trained experts who have no interest in character analysis. They are concerned with the technical and forensic analysis in fraud or forgery cases, and may be required to give evidence in a court of law. Very few of these specialists are approved by the Law Society.

The calligrapher is a master of fine writing. He or she can create certain pen strokes which appear at first to be quite simple. Further enquiry proves the opposite: it is a challenging and difficult art that takes time and patience to perfect and usually requires a degree of natural talent and artistic skill for success. The uses of calligraphy are many: announcements, brochures, certificates, memorials, scrolls and testimonials are but a few.

Graphologists use handwriting to further knowledge of others as well as themselves. Frequently employed by business organizations in matters of personnel selection, graphologists are used to assess employees for a variety of reasons.

Marriage-guidance counsellors may also be trained to determine the degree of compatibility between prospective divorcees, much as single folk may wish to discover potential risks in their relationships prior to marriage.

Child-guidance clinics may use specialists to analyse the writing of a child for clues that may reveal tendencies quite unsuspected by parents or teachers.

There are few areas of behavioural science where handwriting experts may not be employed.

By explaining a little in this introduction about what handwriting analysis is and what is required to utilize it, I have tried to whet your appetite for what is to come. You will have all the necessary information should you choose to take the subject further and experiment for yourself.

I think you will.

1

Slant: The Writing Slope

Handwriting develops throughout childhood almost from the first days at primary school until the student leaves at sixteen or older. Individual abilities are established at more or less the same time, particularly if teachers are astute enough to ensure that their charges progress in such a way that no one gets left too far behind. However, this is not always the case. Where one child will strive to do his best to write as nicely as possible, another may rush, producing a distorted form of what is expected.

Below is an example of one of a variety of first alphabets as taught in most primary schools in the United Kingdom. This print-script system is easy to learn and precedes natural basic cursive writing.

a b c d e f g h i j

k l m n o p q r s

t u v w x y z

As children we begin to develop a distinctive style of our own, but one that will not be fully in evidence until the writing exercise is a normal and unconscious natural habit. As time progresses we begin to pick up speed and bring in modifications to suit (and reflect) our personal temperament. We may modify handwriting by eliminating some of the loops; we may introduce certain elaborations: added curlicues to capital letters, for example.

Slowly, steadily, we progress.

Puberty will certainly bring more changes, but by the age of sixteen we will have established a style by which we may be recognized.

Usually, we write in a straight line from left to right across a page. When we come to the right-hand side we leave a space below the line and repeat the process continually until the page is filled or correspondence is ended. We will adopt a particular angle of script to this base-line: reclined, vertical, or inclined. The degree of the slant of the writing may be assessed from the illustration below.

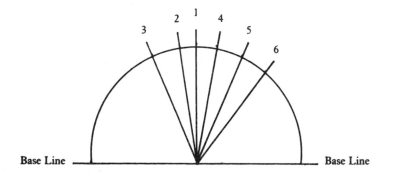

Key:

1 Self control and independence.
2 Caution and repression.
3 Introversion and lack of involvement.
4 Self reliance and action.
5 Emotional extroversion.
6 Impulsive and intense.

Letter slope

The angle, or slant, of writing is the outward expression of the inner feelings, the emotional response of the writer. There is often a variation between two of these illustrated guidelines which may be considered quite normal.

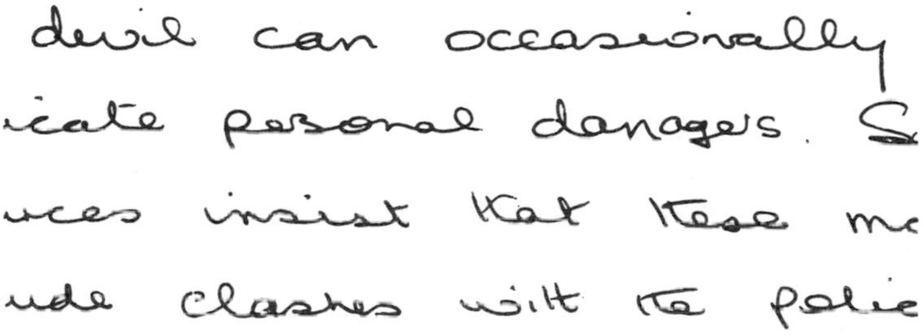

devil can occasionally
icate personal damages. S
uces insist that these m
ude clashes with the police

Occasionally, the slant is the same throughout, with no variation. This suggests that more than average control is being exercised by the writer.

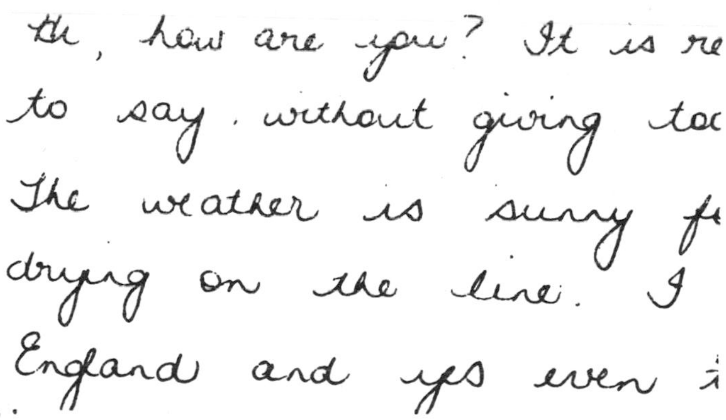

th, how are you? It is re
to say . without giving too
The weather is sunny f
drying on the line. I
England and yes even i

If the slant should range between more than two of these positions the writer's natural impulses may be considered unstable.

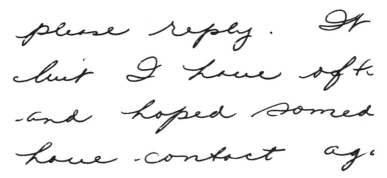

Inclined writing

Writing that slants to the right is the style most usually encountered. The letters lean forward in the direction of the writing movement. It is the easiest and most natural angle to adopt. Basically demonstrative and affectionate, these writers are gregarious and extrovert. Social life and relationships mean a lot to them. These writers will find jobs that will bring them into contact with people.

The more moderate the angle from the vertical, the more self-reliant the personality. There will be a good deal of controlled action. Overall, they are quite confident.

14

and also for the gift vouchers.
shaver is coming towards the
life (perhaps you knew this!)

Too much of an angle suggests an impulsive character. The nature is more intense and can be erratic. There is often a false impression of self-confidence: it should be regarded as surface bluff.

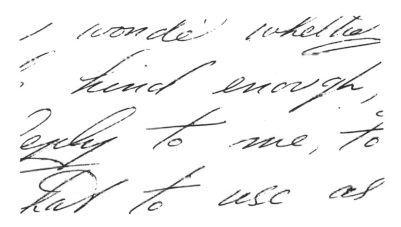

Forward-sloping handwriting indicates a personality more ready and able to communicate and enjoy life free of hang-ups. There is less resistance to stress and the pressures of working life. Such writers will choose occupations that have little toil and exertion. They thrive on variety and change, show initiative and enterprise. Feelings are always strong; often they love and hate with equal intensity.

Extremely inclined handwriting points to extremes of emotional response and action. Impulsive emotionally and physically, these writers are very intense and susceptible to outside influences.

Easily sidetracked, they are basically unstable and may be in need of counsel. It can be difficult to predict their reactions in certain circumstances.

Sometimes a writer may begin a message with good control, then become involved to such an extent that it is easy to see where the writing changes showing the change.

I Thought it would be a
very good idea to
follow on.

This may be reversed. A note may be dashed off, but, halfway through, the writer remembers to exercise greater control.

Do you suppose for one moment
You are going to dictate to me
when it is me that is going to

A sudden change of slope on a word or series of words which may be connected in some sense may reflect unease, discomfort or repression, or the writer may be telling a lie.

Please believe me when I say,
I love you, you mean so
to me. I cannot think of

One word may slope forward more than usual, implying extra intensity. This may be either physical or emotional.

Vertical writing

Independence and self-control are the main characteristics shown by consistently upright or vertical handwriting. There is always a degree of caution and reserve. Judgement is a considered affair every time. These writers may be relied upon to keep their heads in any emergency. They dislike losing control, and when they do, they quickly try to regain the status quo. They are not cold so much as reluctant to relax in the company of others.

It is rare to find writing that is consistently vertical. There is usually a variation of about five degrees either way. The very slightly forward degree shows more self-reliance and inclination to action.

r the Birth charts receiv
unfortunately one chart
think you will find, if y
y previous letter to hand,

Handwriting that reclines slightly from the vertical (by about five degrees or so) indicates repression and caution.

done before but it wi
omputer – interesting t
so. I'm listening to
hi-fi Hitachi stereo. (

All these writers are temperamentally suited to positions of authority and responsibility. They may be part of a team, but they much prefer to work on their own.

Upright handwriting suggests a head-over-heart attitude. Such folk are more open to everyday experiences. The degree of emotion may be further determined by the pressure and speed of the writing. The heavier the pressure, the more intense the emotional side of the nature.

nd enclosed, payment
nistry analysis.
male and I was

The lighter the pressure in vertical writing, the more impressionable and sensitive the personality suggested by this style. These folk are not unknown to have short, sharp bursts of temper when things get the better of them.

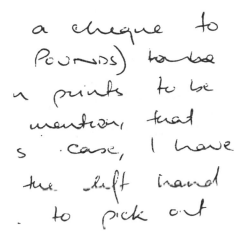

Reclined writing

Backward-sloping handwriting may be taken as an outward manifestation of inner rebellion. No formal school of writing anywhere advocates this leftward slope. This style may therefore be adopted by those who display an attitude of defiance, rebelliousness or defensiveness which may be directed against everything and everyone.

Some associate leftward slant with left-handedness. In many cases left-handed people do tend to adopt this style, but it may be due to poor posture in the writing position. Right-handed people who use this slope are far more in the majority.

The leftward slant implies the introvert. There is little spontaneity: these people hold back and hide their real feelings and thoughts from those around them. They are born actors. They show a smooth and controlled outward picture to the world, while inwardly longing to be different. They are reluctant to show emotion, even to those close to them. They are restrained: they feel they cannot trust. They have few close friends, preferring a wide-ranging circle of acquaintances.

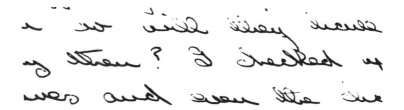

Very reclined handwriting shows poor adaptability and there may be a difficulty in overtly expressing emotion. Deeply emotional, sensitive to a fault, such writers are often quite lonely people reluctant to become involved with others. Anything new will be treated with suspicion, for they consider that the tried and trusted should suffice.

Line slope
The way a line is written across a page is a clue to the general disposition of the writer at the time of writing. (This is one of the reasons why we prefer to have our samples on unlined paper.)

A constant, even base-line repeated over and over again across the page reveals control of emotions. There is reason, reliability and an even temperament. The writer may also be dull and uninteresting.

*until I opened it,
read the return ad...
so excited as I. Peter
little to be desired.*

A very straight line with no fluctuation at all, or one where a ruler has obviously been used, suggests an unnatural curb or control of emotion. Personal discipline will mark the personality. There may be a fear of losing control, narrow-mindedness, repression and a calculating attitude.

*the further interngration
Bureau into the
nistrative structure*

A reasonably steady flow with some flexibility in the line shows good adaptability. There will also be a balanced view of life.

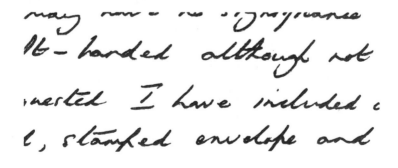

*may now... no ...significance
16 - handed although not
...nested I have included...
l, stamped envelope and*

The writing may begin level but arch upward and then descend to the (imaginary) base-line. Much is begun with enthusiasm and optimism but the writer will soon tire. A lot of little projects get started but few ever get finished properly, if at all.

thought it was extremely sporti
wing as you did that we were
the brink of total disintegrata
that we all learned someth

Handwriting that forms a dish or concave effect over the page implies a slow starter. There is too much caution, a lack of confidence, though this may ease once the task is under way. The writer will finish in a more buoyant frame of mind. Usually, one may rely on this type to finish what they have started.

writing please. Sorry abou
envelope enclosing everyth
did not read the reques.

A wavy base-line shows a strong response to outside influences, for these writers are easily side-tracked. There is a lot of energy which is rarely correctly channelled. Talent may often go to waste.

address. I am male, aged 23, a
. My hobbies include playing gu
've been playing guitar for ol

A highly erratic base-line shows instability, indecision, and inconsistency. Not always trustworthy, these writers are opportunists and respond too readily to the mood of the moment.

magazine for astrology
occult. Please send me
report of my handwriti

When the script follows a regular ascending pattern over the page, it is an indication of optimism. There is a good enthusiastic attitude to life. Little gets these writers down and they tend to bounce back from setbacks with fair resilience.

important than the printed
the printed word, as one
, seen of little use, but
. Why don't I live in
- That is the question.

Handwriting that consistently falls below the base-line is usually indicative of the mood of the moment. The writer may be tired or dispirited. Pessimism, despondency and apathy will also be present.

'd like to know
I am forwarding
with two others
ld like returned
re envelope.

Word slope
At first glance a sample of script may appear to be even, but closer inspection may show that the individual words have been written in a sloping manner. In fact, each word descends. (It is rare to find a sample where each word ascends.) People who write in this manner need to be actively encouraged, for they lack self-confidence and seek constant reassurance. Should this not be forthcoming, they will become depressed and in extreme cases worry themselves into illness.

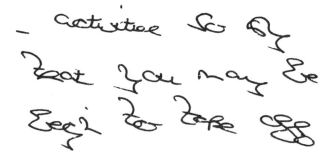

Overall appearance

Even when paper is lined, many writers have difficulty in keeping their script level, but this should not be given undue relevance. A fairly flexible line represents a fairly flexible outlook.

Note the whole sample for progressive variation in the slope of the handwriting. Any attempt to hide the writer's natural inclinations, for whatever reasons, will become apparent when you compare the end of the writing with the beginning. A careful start, slipping standards in the middle, and a return to the carefulness at the end reveal a cautious type of person who does try to maintain an even approach. This shows a sense of responsibility, whatever the overall style of handwriting may imply. A careful start with progressively slipping standards implies exactly that, a lack of consistent attention to detail and poor ability to follow through.

2

Zones of Handwriting: Letter Balance

No matter how brief a sample may be, a graphologist will analyse the script in terms of zonal assessment. Traditionally, handwriting may be divided into three vertical zones: upper, middle and lower. Equally, it may be assessed in terms of horizontal expansion: narrow, medium or wide.

Vertical zones

Each letter will occupy one or more of these zones and assumes a greater or lesser importance accordingly. There is one exception in the true sense: the letter **f**. This is the only tri-zonal letter which always extends from the upper, through the middle, to the lower zone.

Each zone has a particular meaning.

The upper zone is involved with dreams, aspirations, ambitions, ideals, philosophies and abstract matters in general. Intellectual and spiritual affairs are the dominant factors. The letters principally involved are the **b, d, f, h, k, l, t** and lower-case **i** because of the dot. This last item is more specifically dealt with in a later chapter.

The middle zone will show the reaction of a writer to his or her environment, mundane matters, relationships and day-to-day affairs. The general behaviour pattern will also be shown here. The letters principally involved are the **a, c, e, m, n, o, r, s, u, v, w** and **x**.

The lower zone denotes the degree of involvement with the instinctive desires, sexual and biological urges, possessiveness and acquisition, physical activities such as sport, and materialism. The letters most involved are the **g, j, p, q, y** and **z**.

It is important to note that when one or more zones are emphasized the remainder will *always* be off-balance, especially if a letter should enter a zone with which it may not normally be associated.

The middle zone

Emphasis on this zone reveals a desire to impress and be noticed. It suggests an individual's need to be a focal point, to be recognized as a leader in some way, usually socially orientated. There will be conceit and a presumptuous air. Selfish in many ways, these writers become easily bored and need stimulation. They live for the moment, and they savour every minute of an experience.

> *the garden. quite a*
> *put up a new fence*
> *last week. And h*
> *it. had such a pi*
> *burn. that I thoug*

Should the middle zone dwarf the lower zone, with few or no loops reaching downward for any distance, a domineering nature is likely to be present, and an immature one at that. There will be an imbalance in the writer's emotional approach which will be selfishly inclined.

> *with my own hande*
> *sending in part of a letter*
> *like analysed as best you.*
> *D*

If the middle zone should dwarf the upper zone, with few if any loops ascending any real distance, materialism will be a strong part of the writer's nature. Intellectual pursuits will not attract. Emotional matters will need to be quite physically demonstrated.

Is it possible for y
kind of career t
? and if so, will

Very large middle-zone writing that dominates at the expense of the lower and upper zones shows a lot of conceit and self-centredness. There will also be a marked degree of thoughtlessness for the welfare of others.

also when k.

it tends to gc

scraggy.

Middle-zone handwriting that is quite small in comparison to the other zones shows a strong inclination for detailed work and the ability to concentrate for long periods. Usually, this will depend on the amount of interest and potential gain to be made.

Please send birth charts
three aus, for which cheque vclm

A middle-zone script which has full lower-zone loops accentuating the instinctive nature implies the pursuit of physical pleasure and a marked amount of materialism. Look to the loops as though they were pouches of power giving zest to the character.

ould Like to take c

— service provided by

e my

When the middle and upper zones dwarf the lower zone, there is too much emphasis on intellectual and philosophical matters without enough grounding. With the head in the clouds, the feet need to be firmly on the ground but are rarely so. Writers in this style tend to be quite gullible and easy prey for the practised deceiver.

Exercise in itself. /
Any way improved i.
fact that your addi

Script where a small middle zone is dwarfed by large upper and lower zones suggests that the writer will under-estimate his or her own worth and will have an inferiority complex. Much will depend on the uniformity of the writing, base-line direction, and slope.

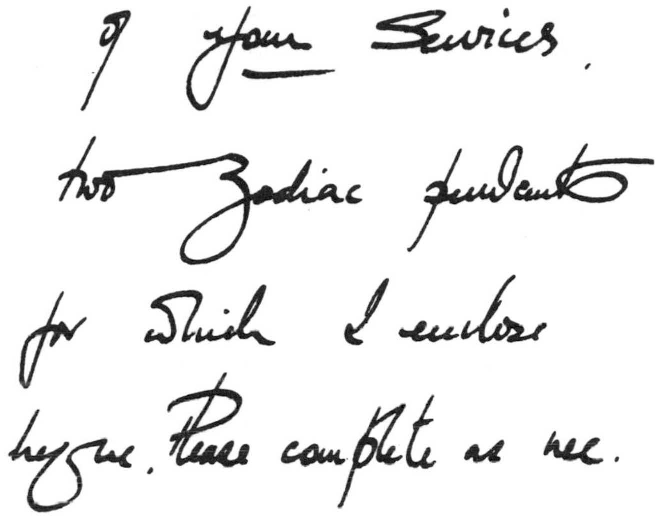

of your Services.

two Zodiac pendants

for which I enclose

hogue. Please complete as nec.

The middle zone represents the ego. Properly, it should have a good balance with the other two zones at all times. Note the relationships between letters in middle-zone writing. Where letter-size differs a lot and the fluctuation is quite obvious, the personality will be inconsistent and moody. Large and small letters together show an off-balance emotional side to the character. Prone to external influences, these people are unreliable.

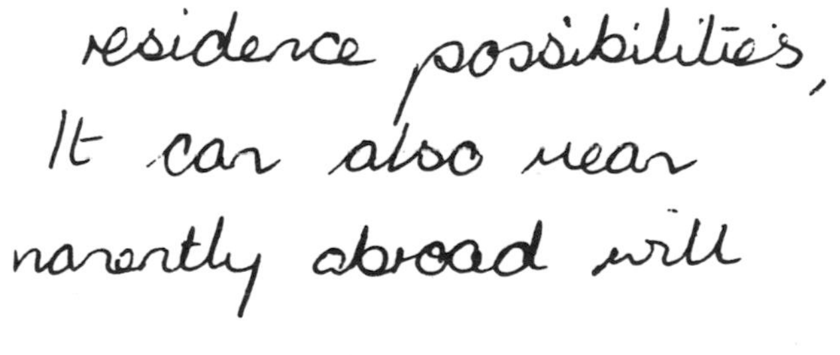

residence possibilities,
It can also mean
narently abroad will

When writing tangles in the middle zone, the writer is unable to cope properly with everyday matters. He or she may take on more than they can or should. They are impractical, undisciplined and unreliable.

The upper zone
Where a script emphasizes the upper zone to the detriment of the middle and lower zones, there will be no practicality and little common sense.

Normally executed ascenders denote average aims and ambitions. There may be no specific direction as such, but the writer will exhibit common sense and realism.

Loops which stretch high into the upper zone reveal the dreamer, the idealist, and a strongly creative imagination. There will be an imbalance between the abstract world and the mundane; you will not be able to stop this writer from persistent dreaming.

Could you please send

A very small stroke into the upper zone shows a lack of balance in mental reasoning and assessment. These writers may be mentally alert but not necessarily ambitious. They are more concerned with everyday affairs and are quite materialistic.

comparative level, a keen upper
We need to have such an
ecause our everyday wi

The lower zone
It is here that writers will betray their natural instincts. Emphasis in this zone shows materialism, acquisition, and a love of possession. There may be over-concern with security in the practical sense — these folk need comfort and ease and the wherewithal to ensure the continuation of this. They have powerful drives, sexual 'and biological, and will be attracted by sport and outdoor activities.

project, cause or
n you are fired with
ve gladness in your

Lower loops that reach down into the upper zone of the line below tell of the writer's inability to plan. There is a lack of order, a tendency to muddle through.

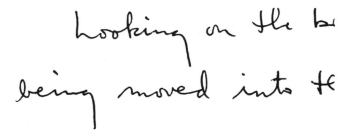

Long, loopless downward strokes imply hesitancy in matters of sex. They also reveal restlessness, some defensiveness and sometimes aggression in this area. These people may be unprepared for the stronger-willed types who can take advantage of them. This formation indicates a follower rather than a leader.

Short descenders, particularly if there is no loop, show practicality and some independence. The longer the line, the more determined the personality may be.

Wide loops in the lower zone show strong materialistic desires. The heavier the pressure and the longer the underlength, the more this is so. Physical activities attract: outdoor pursuits, sport, gardening, etc.

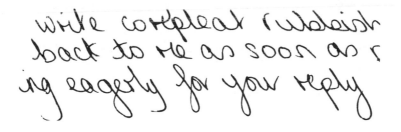

A variety of "tails" — loops, heavy downward strokes, stick-like lines, or even the occasional absence of a descender — shows inconsistency of approach to everyday matters. Provided that this does not spoil the overall uniformity of the writing, these people cope after a fashion. Excessive changes and different accentuations in the lower zone point to the writer's inability to act rationally and respond properly. These folk are very easily side-tracked, especially in the pursuit of pleasure.

Horizontal zones
Writing may be narrow, medium or wide. This horizontal zoning more specifically belongs to a consideration of the size of writing. However, I have always felt that reaching upward and downward

may also be conditioned by the writer contracting or expanding the script.

To test a script for narrow, medium, or wide writing look to the letter **n**. A medium-size **n** will look like a little square. In narrow writing this is forced into an upright oblong; wide writing will extend the **n** into a horizontal version.

Narrow writing suggests inhibitions and inner insecurity. There is a reserve, a reluctance to share or join in. These writers are basically shy.

Medium-sized handwriting suggests contentment with one's lot.

Wide handwriting implies extravagance. There will be added selfishness if the writing seems angular, but generosity if the writing is rounded. There may be a lack of consideration for others. The personality will be quite outgoing and extrovert. In some ways personal discipline will seem to be absent; in others it may be quite marked. Such folk are a law unto themselves.

while at school and
now consider my.
thing" and "nothing"

3

Pressure, Size and Spacing

In handwriting, pressure, size and spacing are related. Pressure informs of the availability of energy and vitality; size will relate to the writer's sense of personal esteem, and spacing will show how he or she prefers to fit in with the local environment.

Pressure

A robust, athletic type will write in a different manner to the delicate, sensitive and timid person. The former will almost certainly have a firm or heavy style of writing; the latter will exhibit a more relaxed and easy light manner. Heavy pressure may often be detected by simply feeling the back of the paper. Heavy writing styles always indicate an abundance of energy, vitality and persistence.

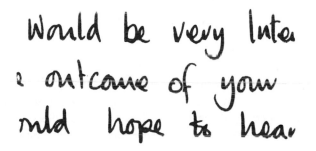

The pressure should be even. Where there is emphasis, it is usually on the downstroke of individual letters. However, when this pressure is uniformly heavy throughout the whole of the writing, irrespective of the direction of the stroke, you can expect to find a very physical type. There will be an air of forcefulness and vitality. Probably boastful, self-centred and critical, the writer may also be sexually repressed. He or she may also be ambitious for the wrong reasons.

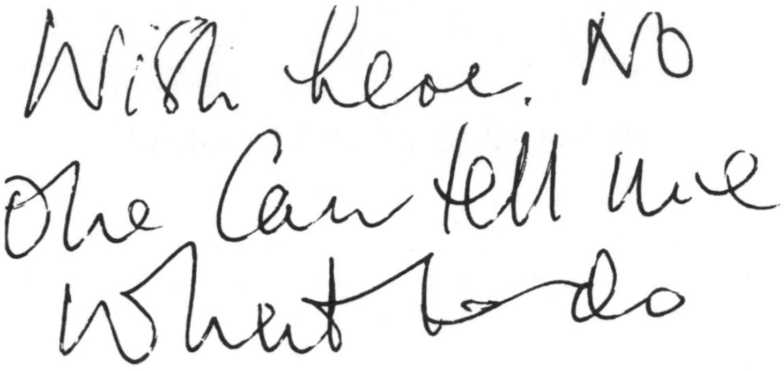

With love. No
one can tell me
what to do

A medium pressure is a sign of a healthy attitude. A positive willpower, emotional strength and enthusiasm for life will be present. The writing is normally quite well balanced.

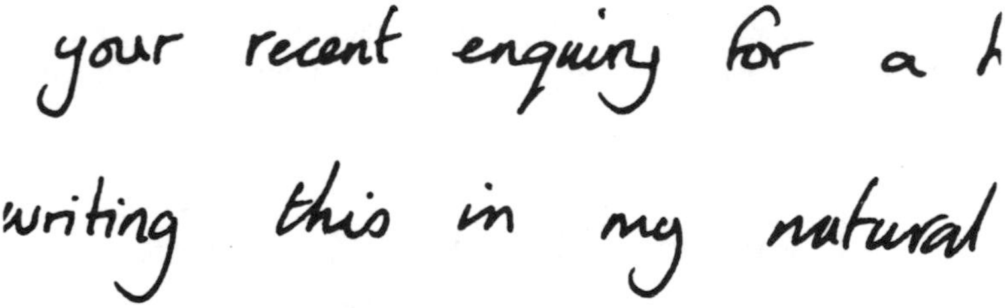

your recent enquiry for a h

writing this in my natural

The lighter the pressure, the more sensitive the nature. The writer will be sympathetic and understanding, fairly flexible and perceptive. There will be a good deal of mental energy but the physical side of life will probably be lacking in energy and vitality.

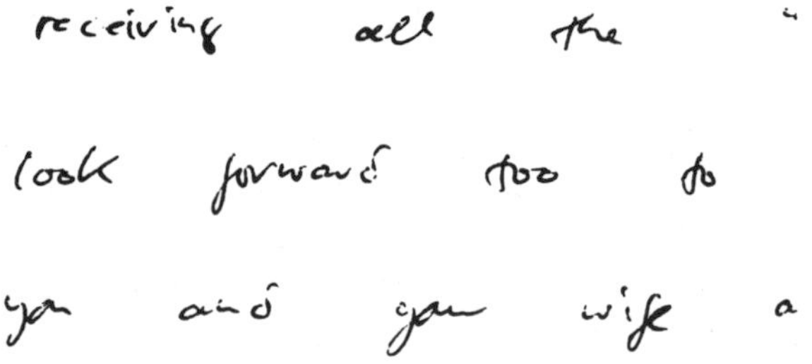

receiving all the "

look forward too do

you and you wife a

Very light pressure is indicative of poor initiative, hypersensitivity, and delicacy of feeling. Willpower will be poor: the writer is inclined to be rather tolerant and easy-going. This type yields very quickly to almost any kind of pressure.

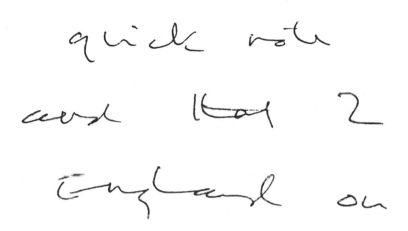

Pressure that is uneven shows poor control. A careful examination of the script may reveal that certain words are more emphasized than others. If these are linked in some way, it may be that the writer is instinctively stating preferences, or is pouring out his or her troubles in such a way that the words are unconsciously stressed. In a letter applying for a job, the parts emphasized may reveal those ideas that are closest to the writer's heart.

The width of stroke of the writing is closely linked with pressure, though they are not inextricable.

A thick, spatulate or "pasty" look to a script may not derive its appearance from pressure, though it does relate to the senses in much the same way. Should writing appear pasty, it suggests that the writer relies a lot on his or her senses, and appreciates the good things in life. Often, thick strokes refer to a sensuous nature. Such writers may rely on physical gratification of the senses more than is good for them. It may be that the appearance of the writing has been forced, especially where a fountain pen or felt tip have been used with some pressure.

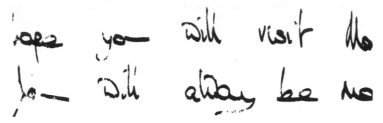

A thin appearance to a script, in contrast, suggests restraint and reserve. Such a writer will be sensitive and refined and rely more on mental prowess than anything else. Emotional niceties may not appeal so much as the subtleties of intellectual persuasion. He or she may seem cold by nature and probably finds difficulty expressing emotion in close relationships. It may be that the writer finds it difficult to relax properly in company.

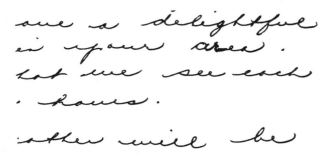

A very sharp, angular script shows extreme restraint and reserve. Pressure is often relatively light, revealing personal discipline. The writer will have a critical nature and the head will lead, not the heart.

Size

Along with the consideration of pressure and thickness in a script, the size of the writing must also be taken into account.

The established norm for middle-zone writing is three millimetres or one-eighth of an inch. Ascenders and descenders may stretch another three millimetres into the upper and lower zones respectively. This would present an average overall size of nine millimetres or three-eighths of an inch. Anything larger than this may be considered large writing, and anything smaller than this would be termed small.

Basically, large writing suggests an expansive nature, one that may be subjective and impressionable. Those who write in this fashion will dislike restraint: they may also exhibit signs of selfishness.

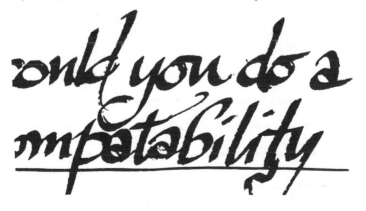

Very large handwriting denotes egomania. Everything has to be magnified, and the writer is an exhibitionist *par excellence*.

Normal-size handwriting implies a practical and commonsense approach in all aspects of life. This is the type that will fit with ease and adaptability into all the right conventional slots.

sn food for the bar. b - Q as much as you want and nine feeling generous. Of your fire works and any

A small script is typical of a modest personality, one who may shun the limelight. He or she will be objective and realistic, often able to concentrate for long periods at a time. There is good executive potential, coupled with a shrewd nature. There may also be perceptive ability but it is not always used or heeded.

Whenever I can, I write with this pen and prefer to use black .

Very small handwriting usually denotes a high level of intelligence that is original and very objective. A writer like this will finish every job started — properly.

. I have always been interested in logy and wished that I had a more fine handwriting. I should very much , know what facets of character are

Spacing

The spacing between letters, words and lines will reflect the writer's attitudes to close relationships, environment and general sociability. We may infer the amount of restraint, objectivity and tolerance present, and can tell if the writer is genuinely companionable, narrow-minded or bigoted.

Handwriting that has well-proportioned spacing between the lines, words and the individual letters shows clear thinking, an organized mind, and good judgement.

His real concerns are honour, truth – and the acute sho ... commodities in the high jovevnment. They would be

Spacing between letters

The spacing of letters within words tells how a writer may see himself or herself in relation to others. An extrovert personality will have plenty of space between letters.

it into the open. Maybe I'll actually looking at some

A more cautious and reserved personality will tend to use a cramped or closed style of script.

Narrow writing, that is, a cramped letter style, coupled with wide spacing between words, suggests a nature that is fairly outgoing and generous on the surface, but inwardly is reserved and cautious, especially in the emotional outlook.

Letters that are wide in themselves but with a narrow space between them imply a personality that is outwardly selfish but which will allow more latitude to others.

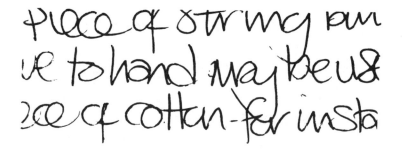

Spacing between words

The gap a writer leaves between words shows how much contact he or she would prefer to have with society. Some people are naturally gregarious, but others only mix because it is expected or demanded of them.

A small space between words always shows a love of company. Rarely happy on their own, these types can be quite selfish in society, taking far more from a friendship than they are prepared to put in.

A wide space between words implies a writer who prefers to keep others at a distance. There is a greater need for privacy. The writer likes to be able to think without restriction before taking action. He or she may appear aloof but this may often be a front.

Irregular spacing between words shows an inwardly unsettled character, one who is withdrawn and isolated one moment, but open and friendly the next. The more irregular the spacing, the more unstable the moods of the writer.

rheumatism, in my wrists
ill. and almost impor
ing up. but luckily.
- me often. It mus
int. to be waited on.

A very rigidly regular space between words denotes a personality which is afraid to lose control. This type must not lose face or they may suffer emotionally if they do. This writer will present a closed front to the world and be on almost permanent guard against intrusion.

ica in 1620, they lande
nded settlements which
te of Massachusetts, nc
th -eastern states of H

Spacing between lines
The space between lines is associated with the writer's ability to relate to his or her immediate environment. A wide space between the lines shows someone who may not be entirely happy within him or herself. Here, the space is used as a barrier between the writer and his or her inner feelings, which implies emotional imbalance brought about by some influence earlier in life.

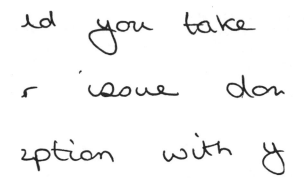

Lines written close together signify a good inner balance and harmony within the emotional framework. There are few, if any, hang-ups.

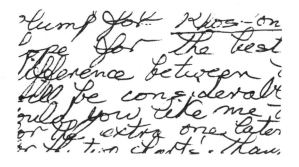

However, lines written so close together that they tangle show a confused inner state. Such writers have a strong need to do things with people, for, left to their own devices, these folk can be their own worst enemies. They are not practical in their thinking or their actions, but are muddled and lack clarity of purpose.

Position of capital letters

A capital letter always reflects the ego, while the rest of the word symbolizes others, the rest of the world. A wide gap between a capital letter and the rest of the word implies a closed nature. Few will get really close enough to know the writer well. The wider the gap, the more this will be so. This person prefers to be left alone.

When the capital letter is joined to the rest of the word or has only a tiny gap between it and the next letter, the nature will be friendly, open and quite congenial. The writer wishes to make contact; it is a welcoming sign. Often, this may be seen in the handwriting of those who have the ever-open door and who will hold impromptu parties at the slightest excuse.

4

Loops and Connections

To determine the quality and extent of expressed or repressed emotion, look to the development of the upper- and lower-zone loops.

The manner in which the script is connected shows logic, inspiration and intuitional ability, but this specific part of analysis belongs more properly with the chapter on writing style. However, when assessing the emotional factors in a handwriting analysis I also like to see the development of reason and the amount of intuition that prevails.

Loops and strokes
Loops always indicate emotion.

Quality and quantity may be assessed by the height and width achieved in relation to the middle zone. The more angular the appearance of the loops, the more aggression is present in the writer's nature. The rounder the writing, the more soft and yielding the approach. Pointed loops almost always refer to a rebel streak present in the make-up.

Upper-zone loops and strokes
In handwriting analysis, the upper zone reflects matters of the mind and imagination. The upper loops will show the development of mental prowess conditioned by the emotional factor.

A wide upper loop reveals the personality which must express itself through the emotions; it is typical of an entertainer, actor, musician or singer, whether amateur or professional.

A tall loop, unusually high in proportion to the size of the middle zone, suggests a visionary type of imagination.

A wide, high but square top to a loop may be interpreted as a sign of aggression and will also indicate a rigid approach. Often the writer can be unnecessarily stubborn.

Irrespective of size, a broken or ragged look to an upper loop suggests health problems. This may be connected with the cardio-vascular system, or the temporary loss of use of an upper limb.

A small loop, one that does not reach very high, implies a down-to-earth, practical nature. This type is not overly ambitious and will be aware of personal limitations. While seen to be quite reliable, he or she will not be pushy: these are the plodders that will eventually achieve their aim.

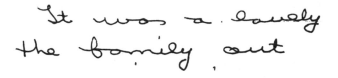

Loops in proportion with the rest of the handwriting show an average, sensible approach. Both feet will be firmly on the ground.

graphology   I   have   decided

A distorted or twisted loop shows a disturbed emotional state, and the degree of distortion will show how far this deviation has developed. The frequency of the distortion will show how much of a hold it has taken on the writer's emotional nature.

Yours faithfully

A stroke rather than a loop into the upper zone signifies a repressed imagination. The writer prefers to experience emotional matters more in a mental way than express them physically.

Classical. G
emphasise pea(
to one scholar
pure form of

A retraced stroke implies inhibition and a need to guard against any intrusion into the writer's private world. He or she may be unable to express ideas and feelings freely. There will be a more formal side to the nature.

ese Oend me a graphol nclosed, a postal Order fe

A stroke with what appears to be a balloon-like loop at the top denotes a sense of humour. Depending on the characteristics of the rest of the script, it may also be taken as showing a spark of originality, although in some cases it can mean narrow-mindedness.

of more than reply

analyse for me please.

unfortunatly, I was

Pointed tops to loops usually indicate a writer with misplaced ideals, who may also be known as "a bit of a rebel". These writers will deliberately bend or break rules to suit themselves.

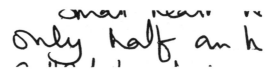

only, half an h

Exaggerated loops always tell of vanity in the make-up. There is a constant need for attention, to be noticed and admired.

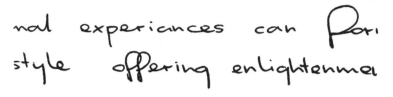

Narrow loops tell of repression and hidden fears. The writer will dream and fantasize, but when it comes to putting dreams into action there will be no follow-through.

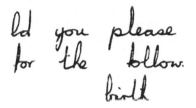

A variety of upper loops shows mixed ideals and a colourful imagination. Much will depend on the rest of the handwriting, for a great mixture of any feature points to imbalance. The more of a variety there is, the more disparity of moods may be exhibited.

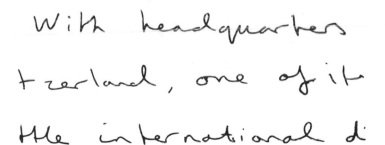

Lower-zone loops and strokes
The lower zone is concerned with the instinctive and practical side of the character. More than anywhere, it is here that a writer is likely to betray natural inclinations.

Well-formed lower loops that fit in with the main body of the text suggest a normal healthy well-balanced individual with average drives and instincts.

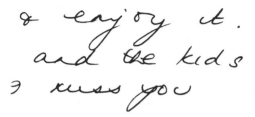

A wide lower loop, particularly if triangular in appearance, implies a contentious attitude. The longer the reach downward, the more the writer will exaggerate, for this is also the mark of the self-opinionated and impulsive type. There is an added tendency to oppose any change or innovation, almost as a matter of principle. Basically, the writer is afraid to change and is only confident on familiar ground.

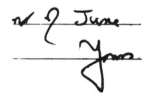

A wide oval-shaped lower loop denotes a down-to-earth character with strong physical drives. Such a writer sets much store by physical and material matters: achievements, acquisition and possession. There will also be a strong libido.

Irrespective of size, a broken or ragged lower loop is linked with a physical health problem. This may be reflecting a broken or deformed lower limb, or it may refer to temporary illness involving the loss of use of a limb.

Astrology is a good way

A small loop, one that does not reach very far into the lower zone, is a suggestion of sexual inadequacy. There will also be a lack of stamina and vitality.

forward to my analysis

An unfinished, open lower loop that swings wide and to the left may be found in the handwriting of impressionable youngsters, more often adolescent girls. In older writers it signifies an unsatisfactory sex life. It shows a poetic attitude to life and emotions. A smaller type of cradle may refer to unfulfilled sexual expectations.

following approximating r of urgency.

A claw-like lower loop or underlength suggests that the writer tends to avoid responsibility and allow other people to make the decisions. Avarice and greed may be a part of the nature, together with a sense of clannishness. Here, a writer conceals his or her real feelings for things or people by hiding among a group or clique. It may be difficult to assess this type accurately for when on their own they may present an entirely different face to the world. They may be chameleon-like.

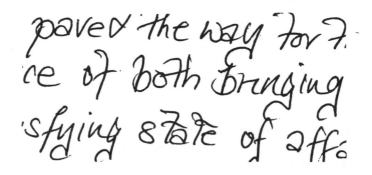

A loop within a loop is common in the worrying kind of personality. This is the type who will pursue matters to the bitter end, often going on long after it is necessary to do so. Such a character can be so doggedly persistent and compulsive it can be embarrassing.

The narrower a loop, the more repressed the basic nature and its physical expression. A display of physical emotion is usually frowned upon and rarely entered into, especially in public places.

A retraced stroke shows a cautious nature. There will be repression in sexual matters, perhaps the inability to enjoy the sex act itself. There will either be too much control or fear, or both. Much care will be needed by those whose partners write in such a fashion.

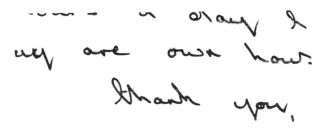

A tick at the end of a lower-zone stroke may go to the left or right. A sign of frustration and impatience, it is a warning not to upset those who write in such a fashion. When the tick is to the right of the stroke there will not be so much vehemence as when the tick is to the left.

A variety of loops in the lower zone shows mixed feelings and attitudes in the basic nature and drives. The writer will exhibit one preference today, perhaps the opposite tomorrow. The more the variety, the greater the changeability of moods and attitudes.

If instead of loops the writer makes straight lines as descenders he or she may tend to avoid the physical side of emotional life as much as possible, preferring to experience all in the mind. The longer the line, the more the writer's energy needs to be properly channelled.

you be kind enough for a friend, whoe's love in the reference

A short light line into the lower zone implies that the writer has a weak vitality, with little or no enthusiasm for physical endeavours.

I am just trying to be very ca

A loop made in reverse shows a contentious nature. Often rebellious, such a writer may deliberately flout convention. This is a character that can become bored very quickly and needs constant stimulation. There may be a keen, if somewhat misdirected, sense of humour.

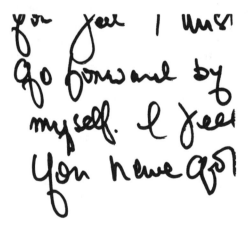

Long, heavy straight lines into the lower zone show someone who dislikes opposition. Although the overall approach is a positive one, there is usually a strong temper. Such a writer may be termed "cold" by others, but this is only a bluff put up to avoid too close a relationship.

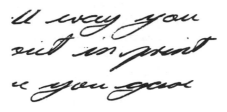

When a lower loop pulls quite strongly to the left, irrespective of the normal slant of the script, there will be emotional sensitivity and introspection. In extreme cases there may be emotional immaturity or fixation problems which may emerge as narcissism. There may be a strong attachment to the mother, or the writer may be homosexual.

The loop that pulls to the right, irrespective of the general slant of the handwriting, shows energy and enthusiasm. Ambitious and materialistic, the writer's emotions are quite near the surface and

materialistic, the writer's emotions are quite near the surface and easily stimulated.

This kind of writing may also be the mark of a physically active person.

Connected writing
The amount of logic, purpose and realism within a personality may be assessed from the way in which the writer joins together letters within words, and words to words. When most of a script is joined together in such a fashion it is termed "connected writing". Such a writer will analyse, calculate and systematically engage in projects in a logical sequential manner, i.e., start at the beginning and continue until the finish.

Extreme "connectedness" may reveal a pathological desire to pursue matters in such a way, no matter what the exercise may be. Where, for example, a course of action by a third party becomes necessary, this writer could be tempted to oversee the action in order to be personally satisfied that it is properly completed.

There is a good capacity for detail, but again, this can be carried to an extreme: these writers may not be able to see the wood for the trees. They need constant stimulation, for they are restless and can bore easily. If left to their own devices or allowed to go unrestricted, they may end up in all sorts of trouble.

Well connected handwriting implies a good formal education. There is logical reasoning power, but not necessarily perception. Only facts really satisfy this writer. Social obligations may be conveniently neglected in the name of concentration. Others may

think them careless and tactless at times, but they do not mean to
be.

Please coul ne my handwriting reversted in one wa

There may be an occasional link between words as well as the
link between letters within a word. This shows good concentration. The more connectedness there is between words, the more
the writer is able to concentrate on detail.

oh May be achieved nore ways than one in ideas to actions ... roll

Handwriting which is basically connected, with words also
linked but with breaks within them, shows creativity and
originality.

Paint the picture as you see fit

The average script tends to have periodic breaks for a variety of reasons. The hand may lift enough to take the pen from the paper. The writer may stop to consider the next part of the message, or simply stop to dot an **i** or cross a **t**. In the main, this is still a form of connected writing but there is more natural enthusiasm, spontaneity and social awareness.

Disconnected writing

The more breaks there are between letters and the fewer the connecting strokes, the more disconnected handwriting becomes. Such a writer is emotionally responsive, open to the influence of the moment and can be changeable in attitude. Such a personality will tend to feel his or her way through a problem rather than reason. There is often a very high rate of perception coupled with intuition. This writer will form opinions on the basis of first impressions. Disconnected writing can also imply a lack of control: numerous ideas are vying for attention which can lead to a jumpy, disconnected way of thinking, and hence to unreliability.

When a handwriting seems to be almost entirely composed of disconnected letters, there will be poor social adaptability. This writer will be inwardly lonely and introverted, and have trouble expressing a balanced social-behaviour pattern.

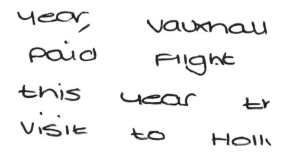

Printing

Printed script, as opposed to cursive, may result from early training which the writer has tried to change. Printers tend to be original and creative but are emotionally full of problems. They may have feelings of inadequacy, which show up as selfishness; such a writer can be quite self-centred.

Occasionally a capital letter or printed word may appear in the wrong place: the middle of a word or sentence. Such misplaced letters or words indicate an unsettled state of mind at the time of writing. They can also show an inability to concentrate for long spells. When these capitals or printed words occur totally disconnected from the rest of the script, it may be a clue that the writer is not being wholly truthful. This may be a deliberate attempt to deceive; the writer may feel threatened and may, therefore, be on the defensive.

So when you feel that I can be of some use to you please call me. I don't like being used though

Printing with all capital letters is a sign of mixed feelings, attitudes and emotions. It is a sign of culture and immaturity at the same time. A writer may be able to display warm feelings but be insensitive to the needs and wants of others. It can be a mark of self-centredness.

HERE WE HAVE A REALLY GO EXAMPLE TO WORK WITH

When connected or disconnected cursive writing is interspersed with printed script, this shows confusion and an inability to think out problems properly. As well as emotional immaturity and mental instability, there may also be poor physical co-ordination.

You PLAN the TRIP AND SEE WE DO, I know WE think is lot & so you should Do all Right.

A combination of loopless and connected script occurs when the writer creates a sudden upsurge or thrust from one zone to another. This is more likely to be from the lower zone to the upper zone: from the base of the downstroke or loop clear through to the top of the upper stroke or loop. Provided the thrust is legible and does not interfere with the rest of the script it shows an alert and active mental state. This is the mark of the writer who uses his or her talents to advantage. The whole personality is very well balanced, physically, mentally and emotionally.

To a lesser degree, this upward thrusting may also occur from the middle zone to the upper zone. It often denotes a brilliant mind, but one that needs an audience and may like to show off. This is probably a writer whose imagination needs little incentive to run riot, and who may have problems trying to differentiate between reality and fantasy.

5

Style: Connective Forms

The style of handwriting will reflect the state of the nervous system at the time of writing. This in turn is mirrored by the glandular balance, or otherwise, of the individual. This may be conditioned by the mental and nervous well-being. From this style we can tell the level of perception, energy and stamina, and overall temperament.

The basic patterns

Style falls into two quite distinct patterns. These may be further subdivided into four main categories. The two principal patterns are curved and straight writing. Straight writing is made by simple up-and-down movements which, when continuously executed, is known as angular handwriting. Another form of angularity, or straight style may be seen in thread writing, but this may also be seen in curved styles.

Straight	ANGULAR	
	THREAD	
Curved	ARCADE	
	GARLAND	

Curved writing is round script and may be either in garland

form or arcade in appearance. In their pure state these styles are easily recognized. However, it can be a difficult matter sometimes. Garland and arcade writing can often be mistaken one for the other. It is not unusual for there to be more than one style in a sample of handwriting.

Angular handwriting depicts an inflexible and decisive nature.

Thread script shows a versatile and creative mind with a tendency to self-preservation.

Garland style shows a submissive nature, one that is friendly and basically adaptable.

The arcade formation indicates a calculating personality which tends to secrecy, reserve and formality.

Each of these patterns show a distinctly different behaviour pattern which is easily recognizable. They can be so reliable that they are a distinguishing feature in any analysis, for they are also difficult to disguise. They are also very difficult to forge.

Angular script
In its basic form, angular handwriting is composed of two strokes: upward and downward motion. It is generally slower to execute than the smooth-flowing curved motion. It looks sharp and precise and conveys a message of authority, denoting a strong will, determination, and dominance. Such a writer will display intolerance and be quite inflexible to opposition.

Although not very adaptable, the writer will be reliable, rarely refusing responsibility and excelling in authority. Leadership skills are limited to getting the job done; the welfare of junior staff is of a secondary consideration. Such people care little for anyone who gets in their way and they will exploit others to achieve their aims.

A square look to the handwriting shows concentration and an aptitude for technical work. A sensible down-to-earth type, such a writer will consider the consequences of any action.

ᴜ ᴜᴀ. book-shops.
to wonder' about
a Manuscript to a
↓ material, and
used in selecting

Angular handwriting with arcade formations suggests a tendency to perfectionism. This type is difficult to get to know, even harder to understand at times. He or she will be quite intolerant, inflexible and critical, and may tend towards emotional imbalance.

In many ways working
an easy life, & the lou
ore difficult it becomes

When angular handwriting also shows traces of thread connections, this implies a strongly intelligent character with a direct approach. The nature is abrupt and aggressive, with a tendency to act, and act decisively. Emotional considerations rarely figure when assessing situations.

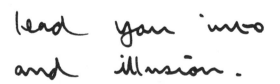

lead you into
and illusion .

Thread script

The individual who adopts this style of script is usually quite creative. He or she may be intuitive and knows instinctively how to manipulate people and situations. Opportunists at heart, thread writers do not easily give way, unless it is to their advantage. Often deceptive and insincere, they will have little respect for convention or the accepted principles of social behaviour. They can, however, be very diplomatic when it suits them.

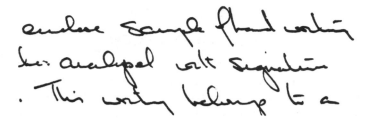

Thread-style script with clear arcades indicates someone who can be secretive in dealing with others. An extremely creative type, this writer will tend towards some form of anti-social behaviour.

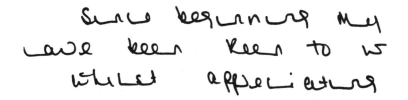

Garlands appearing in thready script reveal poor staying-power and little resistance. The writer is easily led, and has a decidedly lazy streak. It can be difficult to get this character to move. However, to be fair, once on the move, he or she will finish most jobs, albeit with the minimum of effort.

Garland script

The writer who adopts this style is basically open and friendly. Kind and trusting, with a warm and sympathetic nature, this personality will allow others to take the advantage. He or she may not try to stop this, actually preferring the submissive role. There are few, if any, leaders to be found with this style of script. The writer is easily dissuaded from any display of initiative by a strong inclination to avoid trouble, problems and arguments. This is the script of a follower: adaptable and receptive.

A blend of garland and arcade writing suggests a more positive personality. The nature is more balanced and quite creative. The direction of life will be more under the writer's personal control. Much will depend upon which of the two styles dominate (although this can vary from mood to mood).

When garland and angular styles come together in the same script, the writer will be observant and clever. Basically, this is the meeting of opposites and is rare. The writer will use emotion and fact in a clever blend of persuasiveness. But there will be no leadership potential; this is still a follower, but perhaps not such a silent one.

reaching out beyond a fictional

Garland handwriting may appear as a series of shallow waves. There is little depth to the character in this case. The long, easy-rolling motion of the writing could easily reflect the character: easygoing, with little control and poor direction. Often impulsive and frivolous, this type lives from day to day with little regard for the future.

cushions, how should not waterproof, the should be tried

Deep bowls in the garland style suggests a more impressionable and emotional side to the character. The writer is sympathetic to causes of all kinds. He or she tends to hang on to people and possessions. Without being collectors in the truest sense these people are reluctant to dispose of anything in the hope that it may come in useful one day.

It's been another emotional last we with my lovely It

Arcade script

Arcade handwriting symbolizes secrecy and reserve in a personality. These writers need to preserve the status quo at all times, being unable to handle too much change in the accepted order of things. Cold and indifferent on the surface, deep down they are protecting themselves and their interests. They allow few people to get close, for they are on guard practically all the time. They cannot abide being the butt of a joke or made to look a fool. There is little herd instinct; each will go when and where he wants, even in the face of opposition. Once having made their mind up, they will go ahead.

this handwriting sample
thankyou for analysing
interesting / enlightening

Accentuated arcades in handwriting reveal a public show-off with a private inferiority complex. An actor or entertainer will often write in this style. Privately, such writers are very defensive. Publicly, they enjoy being in the limelight. They are instinctive and intuitive to an extent, but tend to lack flexibility.

cat pat on
mat

The smaller the arcade, the more the writer may exhibit inflexibility. There can be hypocrisy and narrow-mindedness, but not prudishness. Such a writer may be very difficult to get to know. He or she will have very few close friends, although they may well have a wide circle of acquaintances.

With some, we feel we think alike we generally have a stimulating time we may find ourselves acting shy

A predominantly round script implies a flexible, emotional, subjective, and possessive personality. The writer will cede to a stronger personality because compromise may be all he or she knows. However, threaten their security and such people will fight tooth and nail, by fair means or foul, to win.

'n't Help wondering what on you'd make of this lot....

A mainly straight style of handwriting implies more energy and aggression. There is ambition and spirit, determination and the will to win.

in London, but I escaped to the country on Saturday morning

6

Form: Margins, Legibility, Speed and Punctuation

Margins

One of the first things you may notice about handwriting is the way it is laid out on a sheet of paper and the width of the margins around it. Before judging this facet of handwriting you should be aware, if possible, of the nationality of the writer since different countries use different styles. Some continental countries adopt a wide left-hand margin for example. Those who live in the North American continent tend to ignore margins altogether.

For domestic purposes, that is, English-nationality writers, the following interpretations may be employed.

Symbolically, the page suggests the environment of the writer. The left-hand side is deemed to represent the past, the right the future. The upper part of the page is concerned with formality and tradition if it is the first page of a letter. This is where, for the first time we put our personal details and address of the person to whom we are writing. How we do this shows the manner with which we hold the addressee in our esteem. On all subsequent pages in a letter this top margin takes on a slightly different perspective. The lower margin, the bottom of the page, refers to planning ability, materialism and emotional matters.

A wide margin all round the page (as illustrated in the first example overleaf) implies that the writer is lonely and reserved. There is a feeling of isolation, the personality may be withdrawn and will not mix well in company.

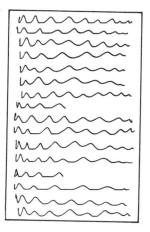

A narrow margin all round the page shows lack of consideration and manners towards others. The writer may be unpopular because one is never really quite sure of his or her next move. Such a writer may be unable to observe basic social conventions and try to be informal where formality is called for. He or she may be over-effusive and talkative.

A wide margin to the left suggests a basically friendly type, though there may be a sense of reserve in the overall make-up. The writer may be known for extravagance and generosity in the wrong things. Forward-looking for the most part, the past holds little interest here.

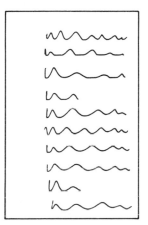

A narrow left-hand margin implies a need for popularity and social acceptance. The early years may have been difficult: either environment or education may have imposed unwelcome restrictions. The writer may be ill-disciplined and impertinent, tactless or too familiar.

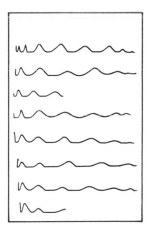

A wide right-hand margin shows a writer who lacks spontaneity of approach. There is often a fear of the future. Such people are sensitive and may find personal relationships difficult. They will probably underestimate their own worth.

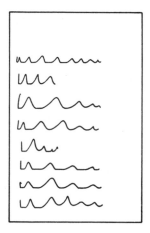

A narrow right-hand margin implies someone who is impulsive and hasty. Full of fun and enthusiastic, these writers will, nevertheless, exhibit a lot of common sense when they decide to apply themselves. This is not very often.

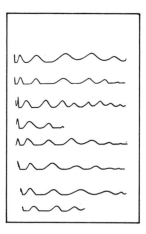

A left-hand margin that becomes progressively wider down the page shows the optimistic and impatient type. Money tends to go through this writer's hands with the same speed as it arrives.

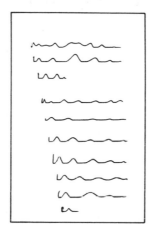

A left-hand margin that becomes increasingly smaller toward the bottom of the page shows a concern with economy. This writer thinks too much before taking action, he or she is too cautious. There is an inability to let go of the past. There could be a marked critical factor in the overall personality.

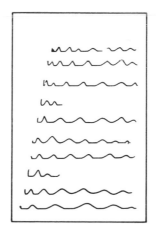

A right-hand margin which becomes progressively wider down the page suggests that the writer may be unhappy with letter-writing. Shyness and reserve will be present. There may be apprehension or a distrust of future events.

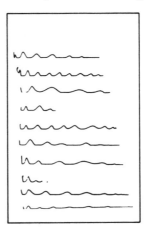

When the right-hand margin moves more toward the edge of the paper as the letter progresses, any initial reserve or shyness may be overcome quite quickly. The writer has a knack for breaking the ice: familiarity comes swiftly in a relationship.

Uneven margins on either side of the page suggests the writer to be unreliable. When the left-hand margin is uneven, there is poor control, a lack of inner balance. This will be reflected in the writer's attitude which will either be defiant or rebellious. The alternative to this may be a form of permanent defensiveness.

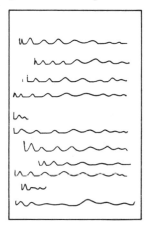

An uneven and irregular right-hand margin is to be expected in most cases. The graphologist has to be sure that this is not just careful adherence to grammatical needs. If this is not the case the suggestion here is that the writer has poor planning ability and is unable to judge matters with any care.

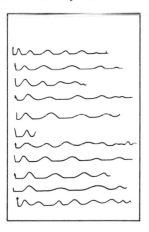

A wide upper margin to a page should be taken as a mark of respect. This is usual, a formal and traditional approach normally observed in this country. It is the way we are taught at school and most of us take this into adulthood as a matter of course.

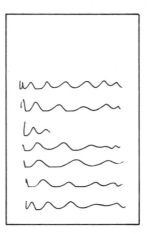

When a writer leaves only a narrow upper margin it is a sign of a lack of respect and indifference to basic teaching. There is a sense of misplaced informality which may have a hint of aggression in it. A secondary consideration could be a sense of economy. This would be determined by the style adopted.

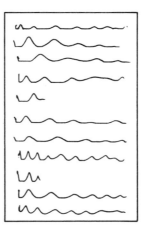

When the lower margin is quite wide the writer may exhibit an emotional imbalance. This person will be aloof and reserved, a bit of an idealist perhaps. He or she will also be brusque and abrupt in manner. There may be some concern with sexual matters, perhaps an unwillingness to become too involved.

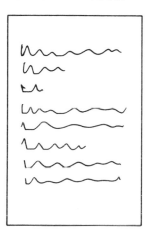

A narrow margin at the bottom of the paper shows an over-concern with material matters. There is a strong emphasis on physical and worldly affairs. The writer may be a sensualist and acquisitive.

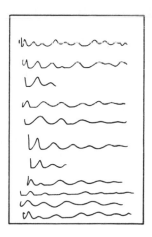

Occasionally, one encounters a script where all the margins are uneven and irregular. This indicates carelessness and inattention. The writer may be versatile but disorganized and easily distracted.

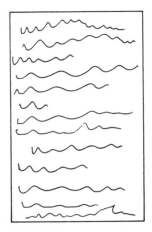

Legibility and speed

Legibility and speed are linked. A script that is quite clear and readable does not necessarily give a clue to the mentality of the writer. It simply shows an ability to communicate. Illegibility may suggest that the writer has something to hide.

Speed indicates mental energy and agility. The fast writer thinks more quickly than his or her slower counterpart who needs more time to get properly organized. The fast type cannot be bothered with conforming — there is a message to get across. The slow writer has to conform; he or she is aware that someone is going to read the end-product and acts accordingly.

Legibility is not necessarily connected with intelligence. Good, clear writing does not always refer to good character, nor does poor legibility refer to a poor personality.

Often, inner tensions will affect the way we write from day to day, or even from hour to hour. It is quite usual for people to worry needlessly about the impression their handwriting will have on others, feeling that others will consider them to be uneducated. Yet quite frequently the cause of illegibility is the speed which has been employed at the time of writing.

Basically, someone who wishes to be understood, thinks clearly and is sincere will write in a legible hand. However, it is most unsafe to assume the reverse in an illegible hand.

Legibility and fast writing do not often go hand in hand but when they do there is a sense of mental energy, perception and enthusiasm. Such a writer will be objective and tend towards extroversion. However, just as easily, there may be rashness, unreliability, poor concentration, and mistakes.

Legibility and slow handwriting do go together as a rule. Frequently, it occurs with a script that has advanced only a step or two away from copy-book style. Such writers will be steady, neat and generally careful. They may also be lazy, over-cautious and have poor perception. They too will make mistakes.

Punctuation

Punctuation, or the lack of it, is a sign of attention to detail. An intelligent, educated writer will take due care as his or her writing progresses. If he or she becomes overly concerned with the message, details such as commas, colons, and full stops tend to take on a secondary value, but there is no reduction in intelligence.

The careful writer who meticulously dots an i or crosses a t is only demonstrating that he or she conforms to rules taught.

The correct position for a punctuation mark is in line with the base of the letter immediately preceding it. This shows a balanced outlook at the time of writing. When punctuation flies up above the line of script, the mood at the time of writing was probably cheerful and buoyant. A full stop or comma way below the line to which it belongs suggests pessimism and depression.

Handwriting that does not vary a lot within a body of script suggests control. Punctuation may differ at the end of a message in comparison to the beginning. This implies a mood change. This small feature of analysis can be very revealing.

Excessive punctuation indicates a desire to show off: the writer may exaggerate or over-emphasize points unnecessarily. This type worries over issues long after they cease to be of any importance. Often, there may be unnecessary underlining of words, phrases or parts of the message in an effort to make a point. Poor-quality handwriting (in terms of legibility, not necessarily intelligence) may be a sign of immaturity. In high-level scripts the meaning is much the same but tempered by other features that may occur.

a few lines of my writing.

" tell you what I look like? w
or is it,- as I think it is-
ription of ones self?

A lack of full stops and commas, or the wrong placing of punctuation marks in a low-level handwriting, implies poor thinking at the time of writing. There will be a degree of self-centredness: someone who cannot be bothered with details. In fact, the more someone suggests a course of action, the more this writer will take an opposing stance. He or she may be quite obtuse, and very awkward at times, often just to be different.

> It has come to my attention that a ~~no a~~ grade 2 editor has been read out a job description which does not conform with the already agreed job function for grade 2 a copy of which I enclose Would you please note these are the functions to which our members are working

Try to read the writing as far as you can to pick out normal traits before you attempt to assess punctuation. It can mean so many different things in different styles. Good punctuation in a neat and tidy sample has rather less value than poor punctuation in heavy-pressure writing. A full stop after a signature, whether the full name has been used or just the forename, always tells of the writer who insists on having the last word.

7

Specifics: Capitals, Lead-in and Final Strokes, Numbers

Here, we move into an area of more specific analysis. Where before we measured the general appearance, we are now looking for more clearly defined and precise detail.

A capital letter may be the first letter of a word or sentence, but it can also appear in the middle of a word.

Lower-case letters, of course, appear anywhere, but it is how they are individually formed as a first or last letter that concerns us now.

Capital letters

Capital letters must be considered from two points of view.

First, look at the letter in relation to the size of the script in general. This relates to personal esteem, the ego. This is a public manifestation of an inner, unconscious attitude, the way a writer may wish to appear, rather than does appear. The larger and more ornate the letter, the greater the amount of pride, vanity and ostentation.

The second factor is the shape and form level. This shows the degree of self-consciousness and affectation. The more graceful the style, the more developed creativity, imagination and taste.

A capital letter should be about six millimetres in height, or about double the size of the average middle-zone letter of the script in which it is found.

An unusually large capital implies ambition and pride. There is a strong regard for display, ostentation and grandeur. A love of position and status will also be present.

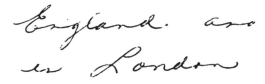

A small capital shows a lack of self-confidence, modesty and simplicity. There is a lack of force, vitality and personality. However, the writer may make up for this with a love of detail, and a good level of concentration. The nature may be reserved but quite conscientious.

A long, thin and narrow capital indicates shyness and thrift. Such writers may easily find themselves out of their depth in certain circumstances. They will be unable to acknowledge such a weakness and may cover up in such a manner that it causes even more problems. This is especially so if the upper loops are also narrow.

Broad capital letters are characteristic of the show-off. Arrogant, often overly ambitious, this writer can do no wrong — in his or her own eyes. There is a lack of taste which no amount of money can correct.

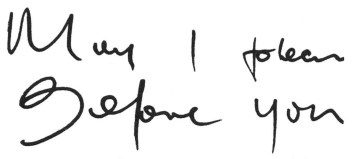

Ornate capitals suggest poor taste and a pompous nature. The fussy and vulgar type who attempts to bluff their way through situations and life in general. This personality is generous while there are adequate funds available, but a tightwad at other times.

A simple capital letter implies an objective nature, and an efficient, matter-of-fact approach to problems. There will be no frills, no ostentation. A quiet, mature and constructive sort who gets things done.

There will always be variations on a theme. A sense of humour, for example, will be shown by the writer who adds in little extras that do not really belong. Basically, a friendly type, open and co-operative.

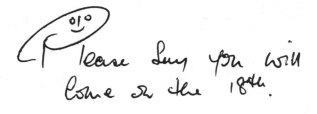

A capital letter that stands away from the rest of the word indicates a writer who will play hunches, listens to his or her intuition and can be quite inspired at times.

A capital letter which is joined to the rest of the word suggests fluency of thought. There will be little allowance for chance: details are usually worked out in advance.

Occasionally, a capital letter will appear in the wrong place: the middle of a sentence or word. Such misplaced letters refer to an unsettled state at the time of writing. Should this occur more than once, it implies a tendency to deceive: the writer may be lying.

You would see If you
So That I con come To see
It is unPossible.

Simply made capital letters which are printed rather than cursively written mean the writer may have literary ability. There may be some evidence of manual dexterity, especially if the writing is square in appearance.

My home
and Reading

Lead-in strokes

The first letter of a word or sentence has a special place in analysis. How it is made, and its embellishment with extra strokes, has been referred to in general terms in previous chapters.

We are now going to examine the specific significance of the actual starting stroke of each word or sentence.

Ideally, you need to know where the writer comes from. Different countries can have their own quite distinctive styles. The modern Dutch writer, for example, will write in a very different manner to the West German. The North American system is quite different to the French, and the Spanish is totally dissimilar to the Italian.

In each country, as in the United Kingdom, there will be the added problem of individual styles as each writer adapts the basic national style to reflect his or her personality.

As before, all references in this chapter are to the English system.

Long starting strokes show a writer who likes to make preparations and conform to standards set by others. This writer will look to others for leadership and guidance. Time may be wasted in unnecessary fuss and attention to detail. There may also be a dislike of change.

Carefully, Now and after.

The absence of a starting stroke is an indication of maturity. This writer can grasp a situation and take instant steps to rectify a problem. Decisive, quick to action and more intelligent than average, he or she will display an original and creative flair in their particular field of activity.

external for

the autonom

abstracting ,

respecting

Lead-in strokes from the upper zone show a writer bent on showing off his or her intelligence. Such people like to let all and sundry know of their ability. In extreme cases they may go out of their way to try and prove it.

Yours Faithfully

A starting stroke from the lower zone indicates problems from the past which may still give rise to emotional tension and anxiety.

This stroke should be viewed as a prop for the writer, like a security blanket for a child.

[handwriting sample: Will you please senc]

A lead-in stroke in an arcade style implies a degree of secrecy in the overall nature. The writer may have something to hide and may not always be entirely honest, even with those close to him.

[handwriting sample: my novel. book will prove to that you can repn]

Angular lead-in strokes suggest a writer who may be resentful of past losses, self-inflicted or otherwise. The nature will be defensive, reserved and critical.

[handwriting sample: No Away Will I Let Mpr]

Threadlike lead-in strokes suggest that the writer has difficulty in making decisions. The nature is uncertain and hesitant. This is the mark of a follower.

[handwriting sample: Whis myor het me tell you remenber th times. mpr any]

The lead-in stroke in the garland fashion is often wavy in appearance. This type is sentimental, warm and responsive, with a sense of humour. These people can be easily led or distracted, especially if an appeal is made to their emotional nature. They usually have a lazy streak.

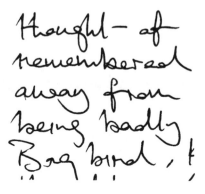

Hooks or ticks on, or as, lead-in strokes of any kind always point to a degree of irritability, and even irascibility in some cases. Critical, not only of others but also of themselves, they seem happiest when carping at someone. They set great store on possession and acquisition.

Final strokes

A terminal stroke will give clues to the way in which a writer will relate to future matters (just as lead-in strokes refer to past events). It will also show how he or she gets along with other people.

Final strokes include those at the end of a word as well as at the end of a sentence. They show the mood of the writer as well as being one of the principal ways in which we may detect speed in handwriting.

Speed implies spontaneity, objective thinking and natural behaviour. An error made because of the speed of thought, or the inability of the hand to keep up with the mind will show the level of co-ordination between the hand and the mind.

This is also a major starting-point for the investigation of forgery. No impulse is so difficult to control as when it has to be stopped only to be allowed free rein again. This is what happens when we write in a normal manner; we finish one word, stop, then begin another.

This is the most difficult act to copy with any degree of accuracy. A fast writer would not be comfortable at a slow pace, any more than a naturally slow writer would be trying to go fast.

Thus, social adaptability, mood, temperament and habit may all be detected from the way in which the last letter of a word is formed.

The absence of an ending stroke shows someone who may not always observe social niceties. Such writers do not need the approval of others, they are direct, self-controlled and careful. They may also be mistrustful of the motives of others.

ing in the book - put
graduation in July
your firm rakes on

A final stroke that swings outward and upward shows activity and drive. Over-long ending strokes also imply tenacity of purpose.

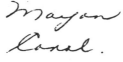

A stroke which curls up and over the last letter shows a markedly defensive and self-protective nature. To this end, the writer may either distort facts or deliberately deceive to protect him or herself.

ing to write to you in

The endstroke that returns through the last letter and into the word indicates an introverted and untrusting nature with something of a self-destructive attitude. The overall approach is negative.

*pun the flowers
in the basket
nobody likes m
myself in this job.*

A final stroke that descends below the base-line implies an intolerant and unfriendly nature. There will be prejudice and a stubborn streak. The writer would be known for obstinacy and an aggressive nature. Not infrequently, this one likes to have the last word in an argument.

*ful if you would
as born on Wed.
· in Liverpool.*

Occasionally, a writer may fail to complete a final letter properly. An incomplete ending suggests the writer may have a brusque manner, one with little regard for social niceties. The personality may appear to be self-sufficient, but this may not always be the case. There may be distrust and inner loneliness.

Hooks and ticks on ending strokes always show a contentious nature, someone who is critical, argumentative and rarely satisfied with his or her lot. Such people may also be very possessive.

An ending stroke of garland appearance suggests an open, warm and responsive personality, someone who will be talkative, sociable and quite friendly, no matter what the circumstances. The arcade type will be less outgoing and more secretive, and will seem to be on the defensive. An angular ending stroke depicts the more self-disciplined approach, but there will also be aggression. The endstroke in thread style suggests a lack of attention to detail, though the writer usually knows how to get a job done satisfactorily.

Occasionally, a sample of writing will show endstrokes that

swing downward under the last letter and body of the word. Such a writer will be very materialistic and self-centred, unable to mix well in company. Although polished and confident on the surface, inwardly, this individual will be lonely and uncertain.

Numbers

The way in which basic numbers are formed should be taken as an outward expression of the writer's inner concern with material matters. Numbers also show talent which may be directed along either scientific or artistic lines.

Numbers which are smoothly written, with no embellishments, show a matter-of-fact, precise and able character where material and monetary matters are concerned. The writer is reliable, capable and basically honest.

1 2 3 4 5
6 7 8 9 0

Clumsily drawn or badly executed numerals suggest difficulty in managing the personal budget. This writer should not be allowed to handle the finances of other people.

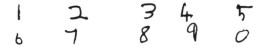

A heavy pressure with poorly formed figures shows a writer who is basically materialistic and quite impractical when it comes to handling almost any type of monetary transaction.

1 2 3 4 5

6 7 8 9 0

A writer may over-embellish numbers or draw them with unusual care and attention. When writing a date or a cash figure, he or she may tend to use a colon instead of a comma or full stop. This may show imagination and a healthy attitude toward practical matters. A certain amount of caution and reserve may be exhibited when it comes to the moment of spending, almost as if the writer is reluctant to part with his or her cash.

1:2:3

4:5:6

7:8:9

Indistinct or touched-up figures show uncertainty or anxiety in material affairs. Such a writer would not be an asset in an accountant's office. Without necessarily being dishonest, such people will be careless and impractical in monetary dealings.

$$1 \quad 2 \quad 3 \; 4$$

$$5 \quad 6$$

Small, concise numbers suggest a writer who is engaged full-time with figure work. A square look to the writing shows technical ability. Numbers that are smaller than the body of the script indicate a leaning toward scientific matters. This type is naturally careful with money.

$$3 \times 17.5 =$$

$$21 \div 8.75 =$$

$$6 \times 9 \times 5 =$$

An embellishment, whether a flourish or an additional stroke to a figure, implies anxiety. The writer may cease the practice when or if the problem is resolved. This is unlike the writer who may put a cross-bar on the stem of the figure 7, which is a Continental practice. In someone who has never spent time abroad this is a form of snobbery and points to an element of pretentiousness in the make-up.

8

Envelopes, Ink and Paper Colours

There is insufficient attention paid to the manner in which an envelope may be addressed. The colour of the ink generally employed, and the colour of the paper normally used also contribute information about the writer. The possibilities discussed here will add more to your knowledge of the personality under review if you follow these guidelines.

Envelope-addressing
Often we receive our first impressions of a writer from the way he or she addresses an envelope and where the information is positioned. An envelope has a special function, for no matter what the content, the address outside is a very public affair — it is meant to be seen. How it is written, therefore, must be considered an outward expression of the writer's attitude towards other people.

In such circumstances one might feel that a writer would pay even greater attention to this action. This is not so. Many writers fail to hide their true nature when writing the address on the front of an envelope.

The writing frequently differs from that found inside. Usually, it is a little larger, as the writer is trying to boost his or her ego slightly and impress the addressee. Writing on the envelope that is smaller than that of the script inside, however, shows a trace of false modesty. Such a writer is likely to be somewhat more confident than he or she wishes to reveal. When the writing is more or less the same size as that of the message inside, the writer will behave in a constant manner whether in public or in private.

Envelopes should always be addressed clearly and legibly. Therefore, unreadable writing, especially on an envelope, may denote plain bad manners. Many people overlook this small but important point and are often quite unaware of their lack of courtesy. A clear-thinking and considerate writer will take the trouble to ensure these details are not only accurate but legible as well — including the postcode.

The actual placing of the address on the front of an envelope can reveal a lot about a writer. Ideally, the name and address should be placed as centrally as possible, though this rarely occurs in practice. However, should this be the case, it does illustrate the writer's good balance and judgement.

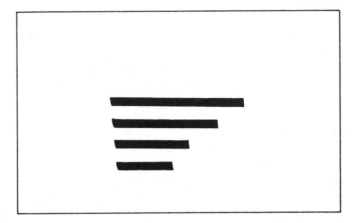

If the address is placed too high, the writer tends to be careless, may lack confidence and is inclined to be a bit of a dreamer. He or she may be impractical and have a tendency to fantasize more than is normal.

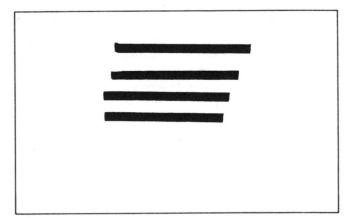

When the address is placed too low the writer is something of a pessimist. He or she is often overly concerned with material matters, setting great store by acquisition and possession.

An address placed toward the top left of the envelope shows the writer to have an enquiring mind. There may, however, be a lack of self-confidence; this person will be cautious and reserved in dealing with people at all levels.

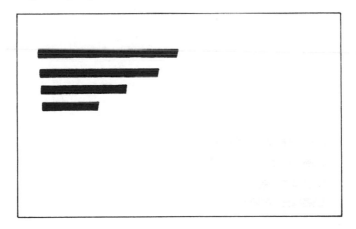

When the address is placed toward the top right-hand side of the envelope, the writer will exhibit a lack of thought and some carelessness. There will be poor planning ability, a lack of regard for established practices, and a love of freedom and independence.

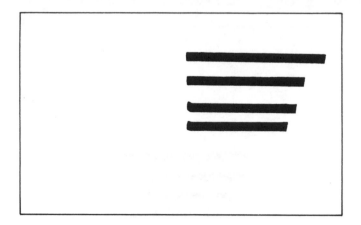

An address positioned in the bottom left-hand corner suggests that the writer is not only cautious but also materialistic. The nature tends to be reserved and there may be a strong acquisitive streak.

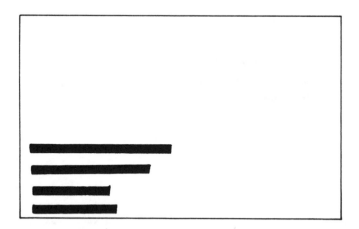

When the address is found toward the bottom right-hand side the overall nature is basically down-to-earth, harbouring few illusions about life. Such writers have an independent streak but how evident it is will depend on how much they can afford to indulge it.

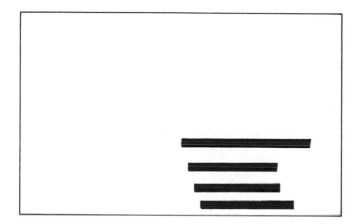

An older-style stepped address, running from the top left to the bottom right of the envelope, implies the unsure type. This individual will be cautious, especially where strangers are concerned, and may have difficulty in communicating even with those who know him or her well. This writer cannot (and should not) be hurried into making decisions.

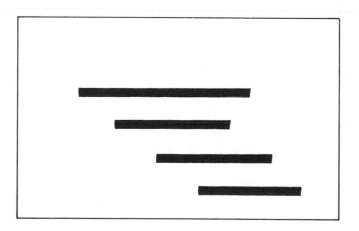

It is an accepted custom in some countries to emphasize elements of the address — the name of the street, town or county, perhaps — by underlining. This may involve underlining each word separately, or the whole line, with or without a ruler.

Some writers take this to extremes, underlining the name as well, or even the whole address. This is a pointless exercise. The writer has defeated the object of emphasis by underlining everything. Here is a personality who cannot distinguish between the important and the unimportant. The writer is obstinate, awkward, stubborn, and wholly intractable. The overall nature is tinged with frustration because the writer is not appreciated enough. Such people are often unable to let go of a situation even after it has been resolved. Such compulsion may need treatment.

It is suggested that there has to be some form of control in the way an envelope may be addressed, and that perhaps it is not as spontaneous as the message which it contains. This is not so: many folk dash off an envelope. Whatever your thoughts, take time to inspect the envelope. The differences between the two writings, however slight or obvious, will always be very revealing.

Ink and paper colours
The choice of ink is mostly a personal matter, whereas the colour of stationery is often governed by what is received as a gift from

someone else. Either way, the colours selected by a writer can have a bearing on your analysis, but remember, only if those are used *normally* by the writer. Many simply pick up the nearest pen to dash off a short note: if it is a colour not normally employed, they still go ahead anyway.

Much study has been made into the relationship of colour, mood and personality; and the way we use language can be revealing. We refer to "blue" or "black" moods. We associate yellow with religion or cowardice, red with rage or passion, white with temper. Green is associated with jealousy or envy, brown with caution and deliberation.

We know the ancients were aware of the power of colour in healing. In recent times we have re-discovered some of this knowledge and have applied it in a number of ways. One is to decorate public places with certain colours to influence people's behaviour. Green and yellow, for example, may be found in airport lounges and corridors for they are thought to have a calming effect.

It is felt that the colour of ink used by a writer, provided it is consistently employed from personal choice, does relate to personality factors and inner feelings.

The vast majority of writers employ blue ink — the most easily available colour perhaps — with the main shade preference being light blue. Blue is associated with outgoing, sympathetic personalities who are normally straightforward and loyal to friends and employers. Pale blue is more likely to be chosen by women with artistic inclinations. These writers like to be noticed.

Royal blue is often used by those who choose positions in which they can care for others. Dark blue ink, perhaps the next most popular colour, is used as a matter of course in many occupations. It is traditionally assumed to be used by editors, hence the term "blue pencil".

Black ink is used by those who must be clearly understood. There is an implication that status and ambition go together. This colour is most likely to be used by those concerned with calculation and precision work. There is a hint of intolerance in the nature.

Brown ink is used by a writer who wishes to be noticed but may be afraid to move forward without adequate security. In fact such a writer may be more than averagely concerned with safety and security, and will shy away from taking chances or gambling in any way.

Red ink is used by those who have to be noticed. There is a love of being different, of excitement and energy. The personality may be disturbed either in part or in whole, there is a poor balance in the nature. Frequently, there is a compulsion to experience everything at first hand. The writer may like to shock and can be a know-it-all.

Green ink can signify a disturbed or immature emotional nature. This colour is also used by individualists who cannot abide being just one of a crowd. Original, creative and artistic, they have to be different. This colour is often used by the young who want to impress, but its main achievement is to highlight their inexperience and immaturity.

Violet ink suggests emotional immaturity whatever the age. With women the colour often suggests grace, elegance and a desire to be a social butterfly. With men, the accent is usually on effeminacy, weak will and submissiveness. For either sex the past often holds more interest than the future.

Yellow or gold, silver, white or grey are often encountered in conjunction with coloured paper, usually black. None of these tints may be associated with practicality, but all indicate artistic inclinations, with not a little pretentiousness thrown in. Yellow or gold ink may show the writer to have some intuition. Silver, white or grey reveals a tendency toward independence and a detached outlook on life. These theatrical presentations suggest an unwillingness to face up to everyday problems in a clear and unemotional manner.

Obviously, the choice of pen and ink is a personal matter. Many people will experiment with colours and fashions as they pass through particular phases, but the permanent choice is a free one, and so reflects behavioural patterns.

A choice of stationery and its colour is also free, except when well-meaning friends give notepaper and envelopes in shades we would prefer not to use. It is here that permutations of colour can become legion. If confronted by violet paper and yellow handwriting, do make sure this is the writer's normal practice before pronouncing judgment.

Occasionally, one may see a sample of handwriting in which the initial letter of each sentence or paragraph is written in ink of a different colour from that of the main body of the script, an idiosyncracy that may also be carried over into typewritten text. Such a writer is invariably obsessive and over-fussy. This can sometimes be seen in those who suffer from hypochondria, but must not be taken as being a definite sign. Similarly, diet-consciousness and fastidiousness of appearance may be other possibilities.

9

The Signature: The Real You

The signature represents the outer image that a writer wishes to present to the outside world. It is probably the most spontaneous and distinctive piece of handwriting we perform.

We learn to write our name at a very early age and it is often the first word or words we manage to master in cursive script. We tend to practise on almost every piece of paper we can, not always just to learn to write, but also for the pleasure of seeing our name on paper. We may try to copy our mother or father, or imitate a teacher we identify with. This junior form of graphomania is quite normal, though it is often carried over into adulthood.

Society and the law recognize our signature as being unique and unmistakable; to forge names will incur severe penalties in most civilized countries. In acknowledging this, we are also saying that a signature uniquely reflects personality and character. Nowhere in graphology is this more emphasized.

However, people will often use two differing signatures, one for business or formal correspondence, the other for more private, personal communications. Caution should, therefore, be exercised when looking at a single signature, particularly in the absence of any other writing from the same source.

The following general features and their interpretation are meant as a broad guide. Because a signature is such a personal matter, the reader is advised to consider any sample very carefully: there are always variations on a theme, and no two signatures are exactly alike.

Size
A signature without embellishment, legible, and similar in size and formation to the rest of the text is a sign of the natural personality. Generally speaking, such a writer will tend to be objective and well-balanced. He or she is not self-conscious and

has no need to build up a false front. It is a sign of modesty and some self-complacency. These writers will tend to behave in the same manner whether in public or private, with no airs or graces. It is rare for them to criticize anyone, themselves or others (unless, of course, the handwriting in general shows this to be a normal part of the character).

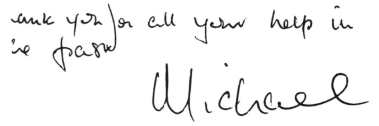

A signature that is larger than the main body of script is an indication of pride, high self-esteem and confidence. The writer will be forceful and conscious of status.

If the signature is much larger than the text, false pride and pretentiousness will be present. A large wide signature always suggests an expansive nature with a strong degree of selfishness.

A signature which is smaller than the text indicates the mild, sensitive and shy type. Such a writer will exhibit some introversion and there may be feelings of inferiority. Sometimes a small signature may be a deliberate attempt to give the impression of modesty and humility for the writer's own ends. Such people are hypocritical and self-defensive, but few of those close to them will detect the sham.

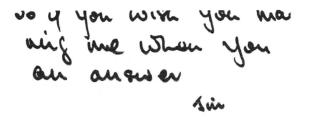

Position

The signature is normally placed at the end of a communication, and may be to the right, the left or in the middle of the page. It may be close to the text, or set well apart from it.

When placed in the centre of the page, it shows a writer who wants to hog the limelight. Sociable and confident, such people like to be where the action is although, inwardly, they may desire security more than they let on.

When a signature is placed to the left-hand side of the page, the writer lacks confidence and is much influenced by past events. He or she is easily disappointed, something of an escapist, and rather retiring.

... y~s in a shop which he could run successfully.

Lois

A signature placed toward the right-hand side of a page denotes a personality that is outgoing, inpulsive and lively. Such a writer is full of *joie de vivre,* can cope easily with most circumstances, and will also recover quickly from setbacks.

Looking forward to hearing on.

Margaret

Should the signature be close to the text, the writer is happy to be associated with all that is written, believes in it and wants you to believe it as well.

...mility that is, for o

Reg

A significant space between the body of the text and the signature shows that the writer may not believe all that is being said and does not wish to be associated with what may not entirely be the truth.

go ahead without him

Janice

Slope

A right-hand or forward slope in writing is a sign of a sociable and generally gregarious nature. When the text slopes mainly to the right but the signature slopes toward the left, the writer is applying control. There is a lack of spontaneity, the emotions may be suppressed. There will be an unnatural air of reserve.

'll be a guide to her
be much of a guide to

Amanda.

If the signature slopes to the right but the main text slants to ward the left, the writer may appear demonstrative and affectionate, but is in reality cold and reserved. This is a sign of someone trying to appear other than they are. Such writers will scheme and act quite independently and dispassionately, allowing little to stand in their way.

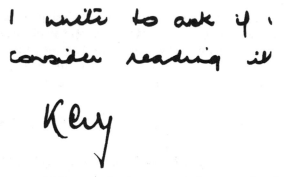

e for his requirements .

Ginny

If the writing is upright, or has a slightly leftward slant but the signature is upright, the writer will almost always appear to be charming and confident. He or she will seem poised and in command and little will escape their notice. The degree of slant will determine the quality of control.

I write to ask if I consider reading it

Kery

A signature which ascends shows optimism: at the time of writing the writer was in good spirits and the overall health positive.

Philip Power

Should the signature descend, it will imply that the writer was tired, in poor spirits, or felt pessimistic at the time of writing.

Sydney Fox.

Punctuation

A full stop after a signature means that the writer feels the last word has been said on the subject under review. This shows an individual who is cautious, prudent and reluctant to take action in some cases.

Christopher,

A semi-colon placed after the signature says that the writer really does want to say more, or wishes to carry the issue further, but is reluctant or physically afraid to do so.

Matthew;

An × formation anywhere within a signature means inner worries, an inability to cope, depression, and disappointments.

Thomas Murray

Capitals
Relatively large capitals in a signature show pride and ostentation. The writer is likely to be ambitious. If the capitals are over-large, dwarfing the lower-case letters, the writer will almost invariably show poor judgement and a lack of taste.

Legibility
The legibility of a signature is important. When the text is legible but the signature virtually unreadable, the implication is one of secrecy. The writer has poor manners, is impatient and may not be entirely trustworthy. Such a signature is saying that you may know the writer's thoughts, but he or she seems to be reluctant to be associated with them.

A legible signature with an illegible text is rare, and shows that the writer was mentally or emotionally disturbed at the time of writing.

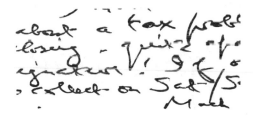

An illegible signature with equally illegible handwriting suggests thoughtlessness and bad manners. Such writers care little for what you may think — their opinions and desires take precedence over yours. They are basically insecure, lonely and not a little selfish.

Forenames and surnames
When signing your name to any document you say far more than you realize. Your name is your label. On being introduced to another person you will say your name in one of several different ways, depending on the prevailing circumstances.

At a friend's party you will probably give just your first name. At a more formal function you will give both names. At a business gathering you may prefix your name with your job title if you have one.

So it is when you sign your name. And how you sign your name irrespective of the content of the letter, relates to your character.

When the first name is emphasized over the surname it shows the writer wishes matters to be conducted in an informal and friendly manner. This may be an unconscious return to the informality of childhood times. (Few boys like the transition from being called by the first name at home to being addressed by surname only as often happens during their school years.) If the first name is over-emphasized, it shows a desire for approval by others.

When both the surname and the forename are used together and both are executed in a similar fashion there is an even balance in the overall nature. Inwardly, there is less sensitivity.

A large initial letter implies self-love. Prestige and status mean much. The writer may have an acquisitive nature, and will take pleasure from possessions. He or she will certainly be a materialist.

A writer who uses only the initial letter of the first name with the surname has a conservative approach to life and is inclined to be formal.

J. Hardat.

Should the writer employ the initial letters of other forenames, expect to find formality at all times: there arc rules to be observed and procedures to be followed.

S. V. R. James.

A writer who signs all of his or her names in full is inclined to be pompous and full of self-importance. Such a signature may indicate snobbishness and pretentiousness.

Richard Arthur Hall.

Flourishes
Many people emphasize their signature with a paraph (a mark or flourish underneath). This is primarily a sign of confidence. These writers are able to cope with most problems: they are prepared to

take chances to achieve their goals, and to accept the blame when things go wrong (provided, of course, it is their fault).

Lesley Williams

Not so the writer who does not embellish his or her name with a flourish. More conservative and orthodox in approach, he or she may appear confident on the surface, but inwardly, can be uncertain.

Yours faithfully

Peter Parish

The pressure and design of the flourish is important in analysis. The heavier the pressure, the more energetic, enthusiastic and confident the writer. The position of the emphasis will reveal the degree of intimacy he will allow. When the forename is underlined the writer will permit matters to be informal and casual.

that we can see

Yours Sincerely

Mike Williams

When just the forename is used in personal letters or in business communications, the writer is asking for matters to be on a friendly basis. In a name of more than one syllable, look to see if part of the name is emphasized. This will tell you how the writer prefers to be addressed. For example, the name Peter can be broken down to just plain Pete, but if the signature paraph appears below the second syllable the writer may be saying that he is friendly, but please do not abbreviate his name.

Emphasis on the surname alone reveals a desire for formality. The writer prefers to control the terms of the relationship and to decide when to allow the greater intimacy of first-name terms.

The more complicated the paraph, the more ego is present. The writer enjoys the sound of his or her own name, is materialistic and often selfish in many ways. Curiously, this writer may also be a very generous person.

An overscore always signifies selfishness and, to a lesser degree, self-protectiveness and defensiveness.

When both an underscore and overscore frame the signature, the writer will be basically lonely and reserved. These people may distrust the motives of others and will be inwardly unsure of themselves.

A double line of emphasis under a signature shows a determination to win the recognition the writer thinks he or she deserves. Although there may be some talent or ability there, it does not follow that the writer uses it wisely. This emphasis also implies a selfish nature.

Elaborate flourishes, curlicues and designs show ostentation and an inflated ego. Snobbishness, pretentiousness, poor taste and judgement are present in some degree.

An encircled signature may be taken as a sign of a lonely and isolated nature. The writer has anxiety problems, is a born worrier and finds difficulty in mixing socially.

Should the name be partially or wholly scored through, it may be that the writer has communication problems. There will be difficulties relating to others, either in business or personal matters. There will be negative and destructive thoughts and actions. Such a writer may be subtle, secretive at times and self-engrossed. In practical terms, he or she is well able to look after himself or herself but will not always do so. There is a strong defensive attitude apparent most of the time.

In conclusion, it should be said that it is unwise to attempt an analysis of a person based only on a signature, without a further sample from the same source with which to compare. However, should this be all that is available for assessment, it may be quite surprising how much information you can glean from the way in which a name is penned.

10

Compatibility

We all need to get along as best we can with others, but relationships can often be uncertain. They may start with a swing, or we can find ourselves behaving somewhat irrationally toward someone we have just met. As time goes by we may find that there is something about the association that prevents it from getting off the ground no matter how hard we try to make a go of it. Elsewhere, an immediate rapport can be achieved. People who act and think alike can generally have an enjoyable time in each other's company.

It is a logical step to propose that, since handwriting reflects character and personality, by comparing our handwriting we can often find an answer to the problems in a relationship. Compatibility is not limited to that between just two people. The handwriting differences between any number of people may be assessed and, in time, utilized to achieve more successful relationships, allowing the individuals involved to maximize their respective potential. Such thinking will bring a more positive attitude from each of the parties: there will be improved results all round.

However, it is not that easy an exercise. There has to be a reasonable amount of incompatibility between any group of people for a variety of reasons. You may not understand why you have never got along with her, yet have always got along with him. In fact, many folk simply adjust for this lack of sociability and carry on as best they can. Not infrequently, this attitude can and does cause even more problems, which have a habit of building up without those involved realizing it. Then, when it does become recognized, it is often too late to repair any real damage.

Domestic relationships
One of the many factors in the shaping of style is the immediate environment of the writer and, in particular, the family circle.

Here, more than anywhere, a child learns to be compatible. Factors to be taken into account include whether parents have separated, and the position of the child in the family pecking order. Such circumstances have a bearing on the way the youngster will adapt, and the resultant attitude and general pattern of behaviour will be carried forward into adult life.

The eldest or only child will have a more marked degree of confidence as a rule, whether that child is pampered and spoiled, or strictly disciplined all the time.

A second child will have less self-confidence and may tend to be aggressive. This aggression will often manifest itself in an attempt to outshine the elder sibling or to prove himself or herself in a chosen field. If allowed, this youngster will find his or her own level and an appropriate niche, although a boy will tend to be lazier than a girl.

The third child has to learn really hard and very quickly indeed. There will always be rivalry between brothers and sisters, and the greater their number the more this will be. Thus, number three child always has to work hard to make a mark on the world.

Even at an early age the signs of a positive personality and a confident nature beginning to form will be shown in the hand-writing. With the lazy child or one who feels that almost any effort may go unrewarded, the writing could reflect deprivation, reserve or a lack of confidence. The writing of the intelligent, healthy child who dislikes routine may be messy and ill-formed in seeming contradiction to the writer's ability, perception and facility for learning quickly. It could be the child's way of protesting against too much restriction and discipline, or of registering that he or she feels he is not receiving enough love and understanding.

On the other hand, a clever child will not always become a clever adult. So, when we view the handwriting of a child we must ask questions of its family and immediate environment. The answers to these questions will show the amount of energy and application put into getting along with those around him or her. When we have assessed this, we must then ask how much is left for the child to cope with everyday life.

Away from home most youngsters learn to get along with those around them at school or in friends' homes. At school, they also have to deal with more adults, most of whom will be compared with either one or both parents. However, children will quickly adapt to become compatible with their contemporaries.

It is often in the home of a friend that a child gets the first real lesson in how to handle new relationships. Knowing that there are certain rules to be observed, he or she will interpret them as seems fit at the time. There is also a process of learning through mistakes. The child adapts, adds to and discards from a growing fund of experiences of life and begins the long, painful road to maturity through adolescence. Handwriting will reflect this ever-changing series of attitudes.

To control the compromise with life's constantly changing patterns and challenges, the child develops basic behaviour patterns and character learning all the time. The degree to which he or she develops an ability to be compatible will be determined by whether the child is basically an introvert or an extrovert.

Introversion is indicated by handwriting that has a leftward slant. This backward slope is not naturally taught anywhere in the world, so it must have been developed by the subject. In a young child, a left slope to the script usually means a rebel streak. Once this is seen, look to the child's domestic or immediate environment for the reasons for this lack of confidence. The cause may lie in the child's position in the family — how he or she is treated as an only child, the second, third or youngest. There may be little love given or shown, or the child may feel smothered through not being allowed freedom of expression. The parents may be too demanding. Brothers and sisters may treat the child badly for a variety of reasons. School life can be too exacting or fellow students may bully. Such a writer lacks the confidence needed. The leftward slope may be a cry for help; though parents or teachers may not recognize it as such, the graphologist will.

Linda, too, for sparing you r occasions. We were too all in there was no lack of apprecio

A right-sloping script shows sociability, an extrovert who has the knack of getting along with almost anyone. This child gets enough love and affection, probably does not find school life too demanding and holds its own with fellow siblings. Position in the family, or the family circumstances do not have too serious an effect, for such a child adapts to the ever-changing patterns of life quite well and will be compatible with most people.

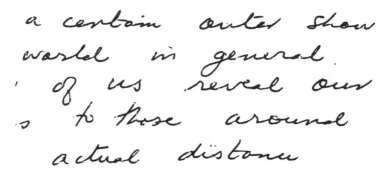

In between these two types we find the confident youngster whose writing is basically upright. Outwardly, there will be poise, control and polish. Neither fully outgoing nor wholly withdrawn, this young writer has developed a niche and role early in life and is amiable, selective and discriminating. Although appearing to have overcome the worries and problems that beset most youngsters of a similar age, this child may inwardly worry. Finding it difficult to make friends easily, such a child may have very few close play-mates, but a wide variety of acquaintances. This is a personality facet that is often taken through to adult life. Whatever this child's position in the family hierarchy, he or she will accept it as a matter of course.

Early domestic relationships help define later emotional attitudes. Once into adolescence, emotions will run riot at the drop of a hat and there may be almost daily changes of mood which will be reflected in the handwriting. The average child will experiment with style, colour of ink, size and signature, but throughout all of this will be a basic type of writing. The most usual style adopted or used will probably be of mixed slant. The writer is revealing that he or she is not sure which way is the right way, which friend is the right friend, which attitude is the right attitude. Good guidance from a parent or teacher will help their child to channel energies into a positive direction.

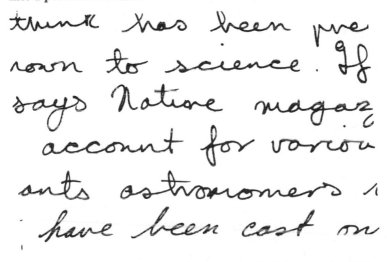

As the child moves into the late teens, all of these early childhood and adolescent experiences will have helped shaped his basic nature. By the time he or she reaches the early twenties, glimpses of the older, more stable personality appear. The character ripens and matures.

Social relations
Because young people rarely forget the lessons of childhood and the experience of the teenage years, attitudes in social matters will be coloured by an interpretation of those recollections. This sense of self is a constantly evolving exercise. It is both a conscious and

135

unconscious affair. Most of the time we are quite unaware of how we would react in certain circumstances until we witness them happening to another person. We then tend to analyse the reaction of that person from a subjective perspective: would we have done the same thing?

Up until this moment we have probably acted in either a negative or a positive manner, anticipating certain results and so acting as though they are a foregone conclusion. When we meet people whom we feel are inferior to us we may, consciously or unconsciously, act in a superior manner and interpret everything that happens in such a fashion.

Similarly, if we are in the company of those whom we consider superior to us the reverse may happen. We quite naturally take on a submissive role.

Handwriting will reflect these attitudes, and an examination may reveal if this imbalance can be corrected. Hence, a sample of handwriting properly analysed can be very illuminating in terms of character. To find out whether two, three, four or more people will be compatible, their handwriting can usefully be compared.

But it is not just a matter of comparing overall styles one with another, for as you are now aware, certain failings and virtues are associated with specific characteristics of script.

When you stop to think why a writer should express his or her thoughts in such a fashion and you make allowances, you are actively and consciously expressing a judgement about compatibility.

Those who understand the basic rules of compatibility and try not necessarily to see the viewpoint of another, but to understand their motives instead and adjust for this accordingly, are among the most successful people around today.

The higher the compatibility factor between two people, the less hard work is needed for them to co-exist in harmony. The more out of step the writing, the greater the compensatory approach that will be necessary. Compromises made at an early stage go a long way to achieving a good relationship. Both partners must make the effort, for one partner alone cannot carry a relationship.

Much unhappiness could be avoided if people were to offer themselves for a compatibility test prior to entering a long-term partnership such as marriage. Small wonder the more practical types tend to prefer to live together rather than risk legal battles later; divorce is unpleasant, no matter how "civilized" the approach.

An analysis will quite often shock — we simply refuse to acknowledge certain parts of our character. However, diagnosis of a relationship through handwriting will show whether to continue it since basically all is well, whether to continue it with adjustments here and there, or whether just to forget it. Total incompatibility rarely occurs, however, if a relationship has already progressed some way. Even relationships based solely on physical attraction have a few other factors involved. An appreciation of the strengths and weaknesses of a prospective spouse as well as your own is the most intelligent exercise a couple can undertake.

The level of compatibility achieved by couples who remain together for many years is based on tolerance, patience and maturity. Unfortunately, the older we get, the lower the level of resistance becomes. So as old age approaches, compatibility becomes more a one-sided affair again. It still does not hurt for older couples to have their handwriting analysed. Compatibility does not always respect age, but age usually confers a wisdom the young have yet to develop. With wisdom comes honesty.

How honest are you?

11

Vocational Guidance and Personnel Assessment

Graphology is particularly useful when advising young people on career matters. Too many people who could do otherwise stick with their current occupations even though they may not derive much job satisfaction from them. Graphological analysis might help them find something more suitable and fulfilling — though, of course, it does not necessarily follow that remuneration will come too.

Not so long ago children were expected to follow a family wish or tradition in terms of seeking a career, regardless of their own leanings. Nowadays a child who shows aptitude in a particular direction at almost any age will have active, but not necessarily positive, encouragement to pursue those aspirations. Whatever the abilities, it must be remembered that basic psychological patterns cannot be altered.

It is possible to study the handwriting of the young using basic graphological techniques to determine whether a child needs encouragement or gentle steering in a particular direction, without being pushed too far; for it can be disheartening to see a child fail to make the grade or keep to a pace set for him by unthinking or over-ambitious parents. Few parents are honest enough to admit their part in the resultant mess.

When we look at the handwriting of children, we are entering the realms of hypersensitivity, immaturity and limited emotional control. It is a very difficult and complex area which requires skill and understanding. A child of any age and development is always impressionable and often carries these impressions through to adult life. If you are in any doubt about giving your child the right counsel, it is best to take expert advice. A careful assessment of potential at the right time can save countless hours of unnecessary worry later. It can also save years of struggle in the wrong direction.

However, none of what you attempt will be of much use if the child suspects he or she is being manipulated for reasons not understood. More often than not a child has a knack of doing the exact opposite of what is wanted. Take the child into your confidence. Explain your reasons, giving the child the benefit of your experience, while encouraging him or her to express personal desires.

Most youngsters have an idea of what they might like to do. Much of their enthusiasm is tinged with a natural flair for the work they envisage themselves eventually doing. However, a talent in one direction can easily peter out without resulting in a career, although a child's hobbies may offer a clue to a potential area of involvement, for children often do best at what interests them most.

Their handwriting should be carefully examined together with a tactful question-and-answer session or sessions. Some may wish to follow in parents' footsteps, others may wish to pursue a totally unexpected career.

There are five major fields of endeavour from which most people select a career:

The Vocations
The Sciences
The Arts
Business
Manual/practical work

Each of these groups may be broken down into a series of subdivisions, which in turn may be further subdivided. Some of these may be of a similar nature although coming from altogether different basic areas. A youngster may wish to enter the Arts, but the particular area which will appeal most has to be determined: the interpretative or creative. In business affairs, real talent may be shown for selling rather than executive work.

It takes time to determine the best avenue to advise, but, obviously, there is no guarantee of the young person having enough staying power to last the course. He or she may do well at the outset, but almost anything can happen to cause a loss of interest or discontinuation of the work. Work in the area may be at a premium, jobs scarce to get or hold on to once obtained. Family status may change: a simple move to another area or a bereavement. Graphology cannot compete here with astrology or palmistry.

Personnel assessment

Personnel management has the task of selecting potential from new intake. This is really an advanced form of vocational guidance except that the battle is half-won because the individual is now active in a chosen occupation.

Managers have to be replaced for a variety of reasons: incompetence, competence rewarded by promotion, change of job, or retirement. It is an ever-changing field which needs a constant supply of fresh talent on hand. In most good organizations, an employee is under scrutiny to assess his or her worth from Day One. Again, good management will see the value of placing the subject on courses or in a department which at first may not seem compatible with talent shown. The testing of talent and the ability to be compatible with others in a hostile environment is frequently undertaken to assess the emotional stability of the individual.

Gradually, over a period of time the subject will either fulfil expectations or fall short of them. Other management forces may then be brought into play. Sometimes a man may be promoted early and groomed for later stardom, but this may include being made to (apparently) stand still for a long period. Management want an employee to mature and ripen but the individual concerned could become frustrated if not informed; even the slightest hint will help in such cases.

At other times one employee may be promoted in preference to another, fail to make the grade, and revert to a former position. It is management's method of weeding out. All of this may or may not be done in collaboration with a graphologist; certainly, the task would often be made easier if the company were to utilize the talent of handwriting experts. The company's future is at stake in many cases. The avenues of insurance are many, and the graphologist can be of tremendous assistance in such matters.

Many leading companies employ graphologists, but, just as easily, the individual may privately approach one for his or her personal benefit and have a confidential assessment made.

There is no set way to the top. It is a matter of hard work, application and dedication, with an element of chance thrown in. It is not possible to enter into an analysis here, but if you wish to test the system all the information you need will be found in other chapters. As with vocational guidance, there are major points to be examined.

Requirements management would wish to see present in a future executive would be:

Reliability
Honesty
Energy and drive
Ambition
Initiative
Progressiveness

There are others, of course but these factors represent the principal headings under which most other conditions may be placed.

Reliability

Here, health would have to be one of the factors under consideration, for an employee must be in regular attendance to safeguard the continuity of the position. He or she must usually be able to work unsupervised, to make decisions and be reasonably adaptable.

Honesty

This is not as easy or straightforward as it may at first seem. There must be an ability to resist temptation in material matters, as well as a recognition of the need to respect confidences and confidential matters. The employee should know how to deal with the sexual pressures that may arise in the work context and should not take part in sexual harassment of others.

Energy and Drive

Continuity of purpose, self-motivation and a consistent and well organized approach would be essential. Health is also a consideration where a job requires stamina, as is the ability to urge and drive others in a positive manner.

Ambition
The ability to look ahead more than a few days or weeks is something required of an executive not only for his or her own work, but also for others and the company as well. This usually means being prepared to work to a point where he or she has established a right to be considered for the next step upward, and will also involve encouraging others to do likewise.

Initiative
The employee should be able to take command when necessary, remain calm and collected in emergencies and seize the initiative, literally, when the opportunity arises, putting forward ideas and taking steps to improve and facilitate situations when appropriate.

Progressiveness
Combined with a talent for developing ideas and the abilities of those whom he or she may supervise, the employee should be able to move with the times, test new theories and plans no matter what the source, and to give due credit where called for, making improvements without losing sight of costs and profit levels.

Each of these features can be assessed by a graphologist who would then prepare and submit a report showing the relative strengths and weaknesses of the prospective candidate. The writer must then follow the best path possible to strive for better things utilizing the information given.

When you have found out what you are really like you may wish to start implementing changes for a new and better personality. Select the strong points and build on them. There will be special gifts, so make the most of them. Eliminate the weaknesses by setting out to be more constructive.

You will become more co-operative, compatible, thoughtful and, it is to be hoped, understanding of the faults of others.

12

Doodles

It is said that a picture paints a thousand words, and so it is with a doodle.

A doodle is a graphical manifestation associated with a tangible or intangible problem, an expression of the unconscious state while conscious attention is paid elsewhere. A doodle helps relieve tension, stress and anxiety, and as a result may reflect relief, pain, pleasure, or sadness. The cause may be social, sexual, emotional, or psychological. We often doodle while waiting for something.

It is not handwriting as such but a scribble or little drawing. Often, it is a collection of lines, dots, squiggles, and blobs, and is a repetitive action. Most people have their own favourite doodles which they use over and over again.

A repeated design of whatever pattern may simply be the writer's way of helping to ease or take the mind off a problem, and have nothing to do with its source. Most people need to do something physical while actually thinking something through.

People who do not doodle — and there are a few — are usually precise, direct, controlled and straight-to-the-point in their manner.

The number, shape and style of doodles are far too many to describe in detail, but most fall into a category which can be studied. This chapter gives a brief list of the most commonly found doodles but it is by no means complete.

Aeroplane

The aeroplane is a phallic symbol. A war plane reflects an association with violence, whereas the airliner suggests a desire to get away from it all. A helicopter reflects indecision.

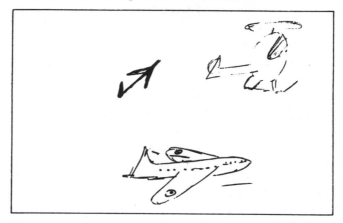

Animal

Animal doodles imply a nature which is fond of animals in general. It does not necessarily follow that the writer wishes to have anything to do with them, although it may be that he or she would like a pet. The type of animal may reflect the nature either of the problem or the character of the doodler. A lion could reflect leadership; a monkey, a sense of humour; and an elephant might mean a weight problem.

Arrows

Arrows show sexual tension. They also show ambition if pointing upwards, or perception if horizontal. Arrows in all directions show an open mind.

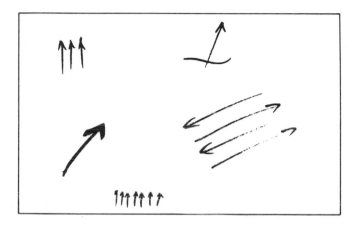

Birds

Birds imply a basically kind nature. If drawn in a series of "V" shapes, the personality is open to suggestion. Birds of prey usually suggest a sense of revenge or resentment.

Boats

Boats normally show a desire to get away from it all. The writer may be lonely. Large liners suggest a love of luxury.

Boxes

Boxes imply a fair amount of self-control. They reveal a practical turn of mind, logical and precise. Should any, all or part of the boxes be filled in, the nature can be caring and emotional.

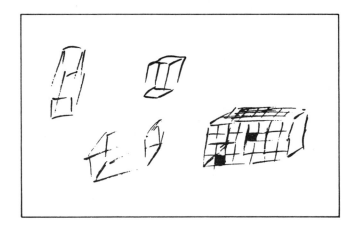

Chessboards

Such a doodler is well-balanced, steady and direct. Usually attentive to detail, they make silly mistakes. If chess pieces are drawn, their construction or position on the board may relate to the problem at hand.

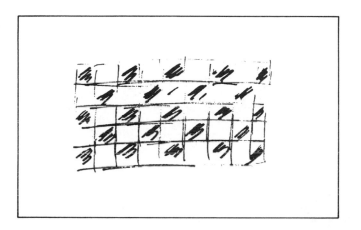

Circles

A circle is a sign of independence. It is symbolic of the female. This doodler may also be a daydreamer. The nature is basically honest.

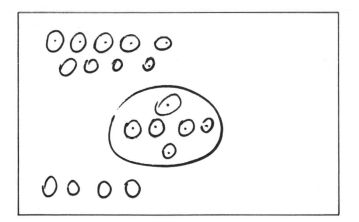

Clouds

Clouds always refer to escapism. When filled in, they reveal deep and intense emotion. Black clouds show an inability to cope with emotional or sexually related troubles.

Designs

Designs are usually something special to the writer. Angular designs refer to aggression and resentment. Softer styles imply a sentimental inner nature.

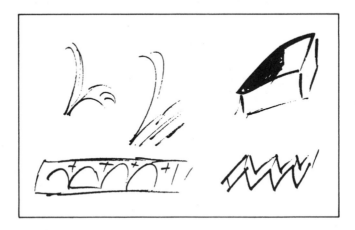

Dots

Dots or drawings made with dots show an ability to concentrate. A series of dots joined together may mean frustration. The picture itself may be symbolic.

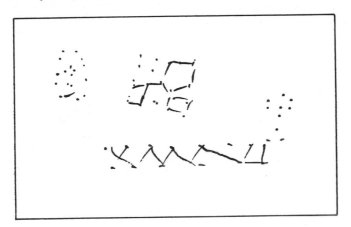

Eyes

The eye is always a sexual symbol. How the eye is drawn will show the root of the problem. Female eyes with long lashes indicate some frustration. Heavy eyebrows over the eyes emphasize the sexual nature of the problem.

Faces

These may be happy, sad or otherwise. Happy faces suggest all is well. A series of smiling faces means a social nature. Unhappy faces means all is not well; people around the writer are not being very co-operative. Exaggerated or grotesque drawings imply a form of resentment. Self-portraiture is an extension of the ego.

Fences

When a name or other drawing is fenced in, it shows a sense of self-protection. If the name belongs to someone else, then that person is being protected by the writer in some way.

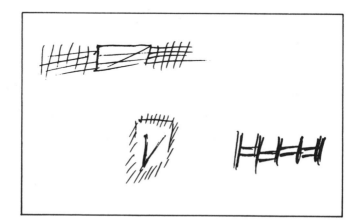

Fish

Fish show realism. The writer will rise to a challenge or dare. There may be a more than average level of intuition. The writer may be a bit of a busybody.

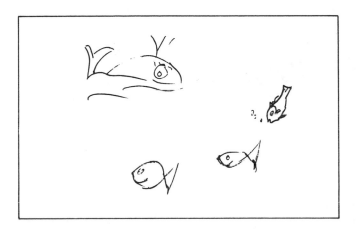

Flowers

Flowers show a sexually orientated preoccupation at the time of the drawing. The type of flower may reflect the type of passion. Often, the nature is warm and compassionate.

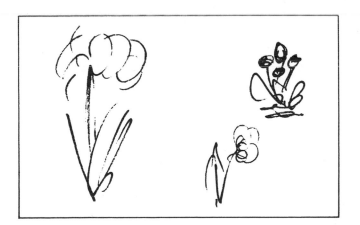

Glasses
Glasses placed in photographs or on drawings of people suggest a degree of immaturity the more so if the glasses are emphasized. If exaggerated in any way, then expect the writer to be a bossy type.

Heads
Head doodles are ego projections. Their creator is either seeking more approbation or lacks the ability to push himself or herself forward. This person expects to be chosen for special tasks but rarely is, this causes resentment with everyone but the individual concerned being blamed. A doodler of heads may be quite creative in some way. A hat on the top of the head implies a sense of self-protection.

Hearts

Hearts are always a sign of a secret emotional nature coming to the surface. A problem exists, at the time of the drawing, with a loved one.

Houses

A house is symbolic of security and shelter. The artist is probably an idealist deep down, especially if there is plenty of detail in the drawing.

Letters

Letters show deep concentration. There may be concern with someone or something whose name begins with the dominant letter. If it is the initial letter of the writer's own name, there is a developed sense of the ego.

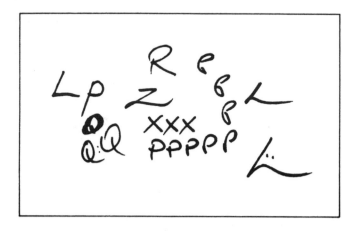

Lines

A series of straight lines suggest the blunt, no-nonsense type. It is possible the writer is too direct and may upset others.

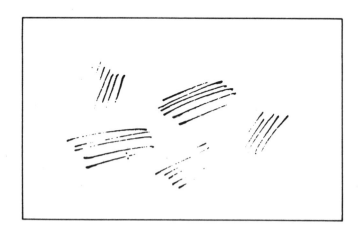

Mazes

A maze usually signifies inner conflict. A web or puzzle along the same lines can mean frustration at a lack of achievement. Often, a maze may be drawn by someone who cannot rather than may not solve the problem at hand.

Music

Musical notes are rarely made by those who have little interest in music. The suggestion, therefore, is that the writer has creative talent directed toward the arts.

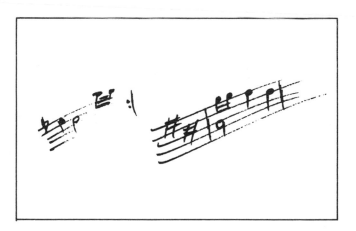

Names

Doodling own names always suggests the ego is strong. Your own name means you are thinking of yourself a little too much. If it is encircled, there is an extra worry, though it may be of a temporary nature. (Try comparing your doodled name against your signature version.)

Noughts and crosses

There is usually a competitive spirit. Pretending to win shows a sense of optimism; pretending to lose implies pessimism and discontent.

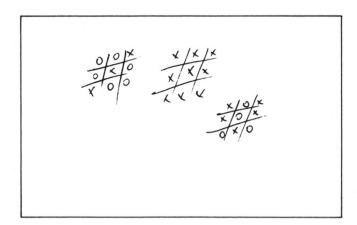

Numbers

Numbers show an orderly mind, unless the numbers are prefixed with a £ sign, in which case the worry is of a monetary nature.

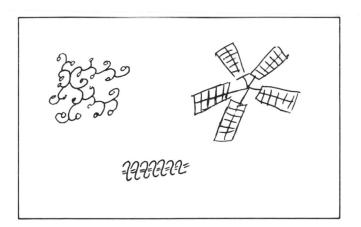

Patterns

Symmetrical patterns show an organizing ability. The more elaborate the pattern, the better the executive power. Administrative powers are shown if the patterns are shaded in part. If shaded in whole, there is a strong sex drive near the surface.

Snakes

Traditionally, snakes are associated with wisdom and sexual prowess. When the snake is drawn coiled, the inner feelings are expressed by an outwardly stubborn expression. If the snake is drawn at length, long and flexible, the nature is probably pliable and open to suggestion. Certainly, there will be less inner tension.

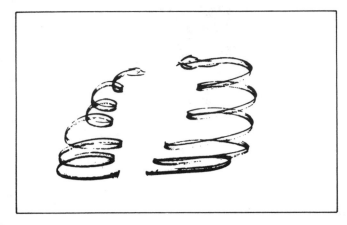

Stars

Stars always show the idealist. Five-pointed stars show a high degree of ambition present in the personality. Six-pointed stars refer to a good level of concentration. If partly shaded in some way, expect to find a capacity for detail.

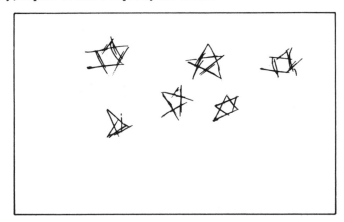

Steps
Steps are symbolic of sexual problems. The more heavy and detailed the drawing, the more there is a suggestion of an ambitious nature.

Transport
When a writer doodles transport of any kind there is an inner desire to escape from it all. A detailed and carefully drawn doodle shows balance and a love of travel — distance no object. A carelessly made picture shows impatience. This type travels without proper planning, and leaves everything to the last moment — he or she loves travel for the sake of the change.

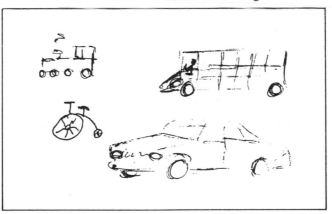

Triangles

The triangle is a sexual symbol. Many triangles, especially if built in or on to each other, show a good level of concentration and determination.

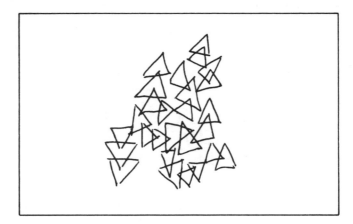

Waves

If the waves are predominantly arcade, the doodler has a secretive side and may be good at covering his or her tracks in times of trouble: it is a sign of protectiveness. The garland version is an example of the more open and friendly character: the writer will be sensitive and perceptive.

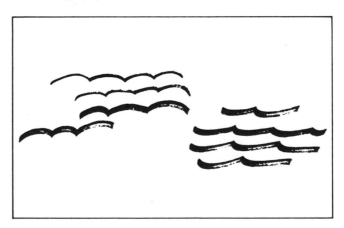

Weapons

Weapons always signify trouble. They are normally associated with violence and the suggestion here is that trouble was brewing when the doodle was made.

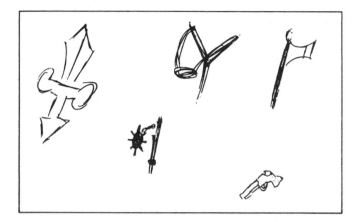

Wheels

A wheel, properly drawn, and quite different from a circle, shows mental alertness. If there is a sense of direction involved, the normal clockwise manner implies ambition and independence. If there is a hint of anti-clockwise motion, the writer is concerned with past glories.

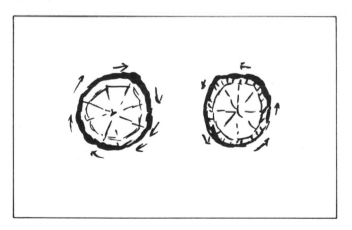

Words

If the same words are constantly repeated in a doodle they may reveal the cause of the problem. Use basic graphological techniques to interpret rising words, drooping words, concave or convex base-lines, etc. Try to compare the doodle with the normally written sample.

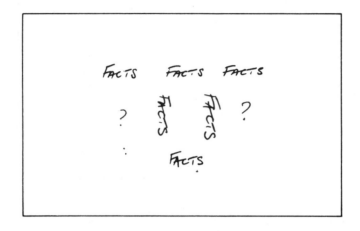

The Graphologist's Alphabet

Having looked at the variations of handwriting in general, analysis of capital letters and their individual interpretation, it is time to turn to the small (lower-case) letter or "minuscule". This is equally worthy of individual analysis. Study has shown that some letters are quite clearly associated with certain aspects of behaviour.

Basically, small letters occupy the middle zone, the core part of any script. This is the area where we observe certain specific and very important issues of character and personality: self-confidence, the ego and emotional responsiveness, self-control, honesty and dishonesty, general outlook and stability.

However, some letters also send ascenders and descenders into the upper and lower zones respectively. The letter f, the only tri-zonal letter, has its special indications as well.

The minuscules, therefore, should be individually examined for further clues toward the overall assessment of character. It must be stressed again that it is not proper or correct to take one letter and its peculiar (singular) formation in a sample of handwriting as being a definite aspect of character. Always look elsewhere for supportive evidence — do remember the golden rule.

Obviously, it is not possible to list all the variations of all the letters of the alphabet. (The word, incidentally, comes from the first two Greek letters — *alpha* and *beta*.) When comparing a sample with this alphabet, look to the nearest in style or shape and begin your assessment from there.

The letter a

The a has always been the first letter of the English alphabet. It frequently occurs as an initial, or on its own as the indefinite article. Occasionally it ends a word. It began life as a consonant, but usage and time now mark it as a vowel.

1 Printed: artistic ability.
2 Open at the top: talkative nature.
3 Open at the bottom: dishonesty.
4 Knotting: deception.
5 Square shape: practicality; mechanical ability.
6 Starting stroke: caution; carefulness.
7 Rising final: a daydreamer; self-protection; possible generosity.
8 Wide: imaginative; broadminded; tolerant; practical.
9 Angular final: avaricious.
10 Final below base-line: stubborn; obstinate.

In an average script some will be open, some closed, some wide, and some will be another type; this is quite usual. A consistent version will show a definite tendency toward the trait indicated. Thus, a series of wide letter a's will indicate broadmindedness and tolerance with an active imagination.

The letter b

The letter **b** has always held the second place in the English alphabet. Its present form goes back over fifteen hundred years almost without change.

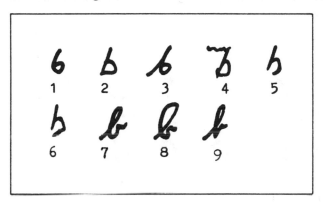

1 Figure 6: good with figures.
2 No loop: intelligence; good judgement.
3 Starting stroke: fussy; if long, argumentative.
4 Wavy starting stroke: wit; a sense of humour.
5 Open at base-line: deception; dishonesty.
6 Open at left: hypocrisy.
7 Narrow loop: restricted, or restrictive imagination.
8 Wide loop: imaginative; if short, egotistical.
9 Pointed base: obdurate; awkward.

Two letter b's together should be consistent in height, angle and size. This reveals good control. An obvious difference indicates a lack of stability and poor self-confidence.

The letter c

The letter **c** was once interchangeable with the **k** and to a lesser extent with the **g**. For a short time it was also linked with the **q**. It has always been the third letter of the English alphabet, despite this mixed history.

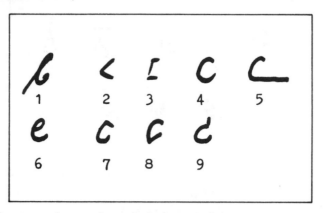

1 Long starting stroke: calculating mind.
2 Angular: constructive; quick mind; temper.
3 Square: practical.
4 Round: warm nature; literate or fond of reading.
5 Extended base: self-admiring.
6 As letter **e**: egotism.
7 Angular top: enquiring mind.
8 Angular base: selfish; determined.
9 Vertical starting stroke: enterprising.

It is usual to find this letter with a starting stroke. This suggests a slight tendency we all have to worry or look to the past for support. A consistent series of starting strokes will confirm this. Written without a stroke, it implies self-sufficiency.

The letter d

This fourth letter has also kept its position since it was adopted into the English alphabet. The minuscule is an adapted form of the majuscule which was developed through the ages from the speed with which the scribes may have written.

1 Tent-like base: stubborn; quiet, poor social approach.
2 Short stem: independent; modest.
3 Long stem: idealistic; strong ambitions.
4 Narrow loop: worrier; sensitive; emotional.
5 Base open: difficulty in getting along with others; hypocrisy.
6 Pot-lid style: stubborn; wilful; resentful; prejudiced.
7 Squared loop: obstinate; aggressive.
8 Wide loop: over emotional outlook.
9 Reversed: rebel streak; awkward.
10 Stem forward: fun-loving; poor sense of responsibility.
11 Broken stem: touchy; irritable; unstable.
12 Top open: talkative; unable to keep a secret; if wide, untrustworthy.
13 Greek form: appreciation of culture; perception.

This letter will reveal how much social adaptability the writer possesses. Study this letter carefully and look for variations. The more there are, the more likely the writer can adapt — but on his or her own terms. Where two **d**'s are written together they should be of the same formation. This shows consistency of approach. When they differ there may be some instability.

The letter e

The letter **e** used to be the fourth letter of ancient alphabets and then became the fifth when introduced to the English language. Around the third century AD, both the capital and the small letter became more rounded and the minuscule version of today was developed.

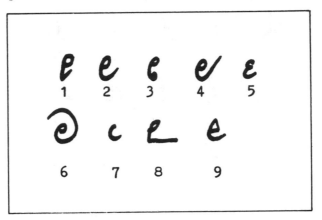

1   Angular base: bad temper; poor social adaptability.
2   Garland final: friendly; generous; open.
3   Looped final: self-protective; selfish.
4   Vertical final: day-dreamer.
5   Greek form: refined; cultural interests.
6   Curled final: defensive; tendency to lie.
7   As small i: uncomplicated; straightforward.
8   Long horizontal final: cautious; curious; inquisitive; suspicious.
9   Angular top: enquiring mind; calculating.

The **e** frequently ends a word or sentence and is particularly important when it is the last letter of a line. The longer the end stroke, as if to fill space, the more cautious and self-protective the nature. An abrupt final suggests a brusque and matter-of-fact attitude which can be easily misunderstood or misinterpreted.

The letter f

The only tri-zonal letter in the English alphabet, the f has a mixed history. At one stage it was represented by the letters wh together. Sometimes it was substituted for, or used instead of, the letter **v**. Certain names which begin with a double **f** (ffoulkes) do so because of the earlier practice of writing a double minuscule instead of the majuscule to represent the capital.

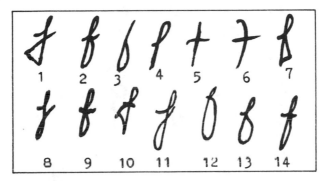

1 Triangular base: unhappy sexual life; domestic problems.
2 Balanced: good organizer.
3 No upper loop: practical; gets things done; energy.
4 No lower loop: full of ideas; little follow-through.
5 As a cross: religious feelings; superstitious; fatalistic.
6 Simple form: perceptive mind; intelligent; quick; alert.
7 Angular base: resentful; uncompromising.
8 Reverse loop: quick mind; perceptive; alert.
9 Knotted: hard; persistent; tenacious.
10 Frogfoot: opportunistic; deceptive; two-faced.
11 Tick at start: observant; if wavy, a sense of fun and humour.
12 Loops pointed: resentful; penetrating mind; inquisitive.
13 Full base loop: restless; energetic; if long, outdoor lover.
14 Narrow: reserved; formal; if short, inhibited.

The more balanced this letter appears, the more inwardly contented the writer is. An exaggeration in any of the zones emphasizes the qualities or failings represented. Along with the letter **g**, the letters **f** and **y** will reveal information regarding the physical approach of the writer to everyday life, including, to a lesser degree, sex.

The letter g

In its present form, the letter g is comparatively new. It replaced the letter z in about the fourth century BC for a short period. Prior to this it was more widely used as the letter c, which in itself was interchangeable with the letter k. The minuscule is totally different to the majuscule in cursive writing; exactly why is not known.

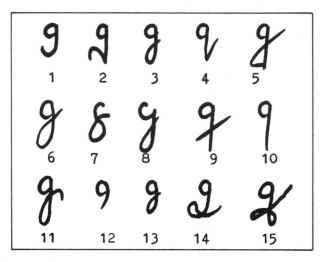

1 Open loop: desire for change; restless physical nature.
2 Arc to left: clannishness; dislike or avoidance of responsibility.
3 Low crossing: sexual incompatibility.
4 Like a q: repressed sexual drive; kindly nature, altruism.
5 Triangular loop: cold nature; if large, could be domestic unrest.
6 Large loop: physical energy; stamina; good sex drive.
7 Greek form: financial resourcefulness; love of culture.
8 Open middle: liking for good food.
9 Cross loop: restriction; unhappy sex life.
10 No loop: if heavy, determined; if weak, vacillation.
11 Hooked final: acquisitive; egotistical.
12 Figure 9: taste; judgement; mathematical or musical inclination.
13 Small loop: poor sex drive; poor stamina; physical weakness.
14 Unusual loop: unusual sexual interests.
15 Double loop: compulsiveness.

We look to the letter **g** to assess physical energy and reserves. The expression of the libido and the writer's attitude to possessions may also be found. A variety of loops suggests poor self-control in physical matters. In extreme cases, it shows poor physical coordination, especially if found in below-average writing.

The letter h

The eighth letter of the English alphabet is largely unchanged from its original form and has always been used as an aspirate (though it is frequently incorrectly used or ignored in colloquial English).

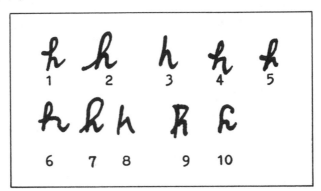

1   Small loop: humour; orginality.
2   Tall loop: idealist; dreamer.
3   Loopless: good judgement; if tall, hard and unfeeling.
4   Final below base line: determined; aggressive.
5   Short final: lacking confidence; unwilling to be involved.
6   Wide base: over-confident; bluffer.
7   Wide loop: emotional sensitivity.
8   Angular: aggressive.
9   Flattened loop: awkward; stubborn.
10 Open loop: lack of responsibility.

The letter **h** should be checked to see if the vertical stroke is parallel and consistent with the general slant of the sample in which it is found. When it is, it shows a good sense of control. Too much variation implies impractical ideas. More than one type of letter within the sample suggests an inconsistent approach.

The letter i

The letter **i** is historically linked with the **y** and the **j** (which was once the capital form). The dot was added about eight hundred years ago to avoid confusion with letters like **n, m** and **u,** with similar downstrokes.

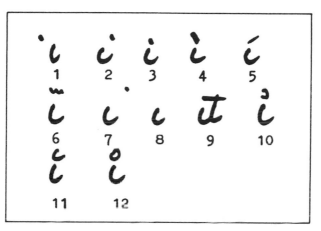

1 Dot to the left: procrastination; caution; introversion.
2 Dot to the right: impulse; enthusiasm; extroversion.
3 Exactly placed: careful; attention to detail; precise.
4 Club dot: earthy passions.
5 Dash dot: irritability; temper.
6 Wavy dot: sense of humour; fun-loving.
7 High-flying dot: idealistic; imaginative; creative.
8 No dot: lazy; weak; careless; absentminded.
9 Dot used to connect: intelligent; perceptive.
10 Arc dot to left: sensitive; introspective; if angular, sharp tongue.
11 Arc dot to right: observant; intuitive.
12 Circle dot: creativity; artistic ability; non-conformity; emotional immaturity; food faddishness; desire for attention; some eccentricity; manual dexterity.

A letter **i** which is consistently smaller than the rest of the middle-zone script suggests introversion, inner insecurity and worry. The same size or larger points to a sense of confidence and poise. There can be as many as five or six different types and styles within a sample, and this may be considered as reasonably normal.

The small letter i used instead of the capital for the personal pronoun shows immaturity, lack of drive, little enthusiasm; one who is easily led. When there is little variation to be seen, the writer is exhibiting control which may not be natural.

The letter j

The letter j was added to the alphabet about six hundred years ago, but it was more of an alternative than an addition. The letters i and y were used as a vowel and consonant respectively, and the modification j came into being mainly when either form was used as an initial letter. Usage became more formal in the middle of the seventeenth century and the j became the tenth letter of the English alphabet.

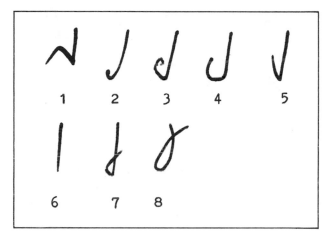

1 Arc to the left: avarice; a lack of responsibility.
2 Curve to the left: immaturity; if pronounced: sensitivity.
3 Hook on loop: acquisitive nature.
4 Long wide loop: easily led; lacks drive.
5 Angular: brusque; direct; irritable.
6 No loop: straightforward; discerning; good judgement.
7 Tiny loop: weak; low vitality; poor drive.
8 Large loop: vital; energetic; outdoor pursuits attract.
   Dots should be read as for the letter i.

Sometimes there may be an appearance of conflict between the way the dot is shaped and placed and the formation of the letter. This shows poor emotional balance and inner uncertainty. The letter j can be read in conjunction with the letters g, f and y to determine libido, physical energy and attitude to everyday life.

The letter k

The letter **k** has always been the eleventh letter of the English alphabet, though the shape has varied considerably throughout its history. Its sound linked it in earlier orthography with the letter **q** and letter **c**. It was only a few hundred years ago that the minuscule we use today came into being.

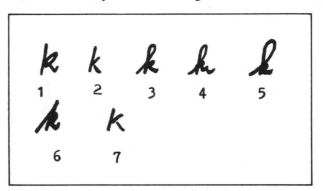

1 Large loop on stem: rebel streak; defiant; awkward.
2 Simple style: efficient; straightforward; uncomplicated.
3 Tall narrow loop: idealistic; repressed; inhibited; formal.
4 Knotted stem: precise; efficient; careful.
5 High wide loop: emotional; sensitive.
6 Long starting stroke: determined; resentful; brusque.
7 Printed: calm; open; creative.

The more the letter **k** varies in a sample of handwriting, the more the writer lacks control in day-to-day affairs. The more consistent the shape and style, the more controlled the writer. The rest of the script will determine the emotional background.

178

The letter l

The twelfth letter of the modern alphabet has a modest history. Originally, the letter l was a simple straight line. The present form developed largely as a result of early writers connecting the original shape to the following letter with a loop.

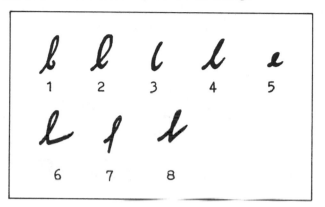

1 Tall narrow loop: idealist; dreamer.
2 Wide loop: broadminded; imaginative; tolerant.
3 Simple form: good judgement.
4 Retraced loop: cautious; narrowminded.
5 Small: shy; retiring.
6 Long final: lonely; kind nature.
7 Endstroke below base-line: abrupt; quick temper.
8 Angular: selfish; blunt; uncompromising.

The small letter l is often written with a loop, which is always an indication of emotion. The development or otherwise of the loop will inform of the quality and quantity of emotion within the personality. Two consecutive letter l's should be uniformly written. Where they are not, the implication is of emotional inconsistency and inability to control the feelings. There may also be a lack of conviction of ideals; the writer can be easily led or distracted. If all the letter l's in a sample are similarly executed it is a sign of control.

179

The letter m

The thirteenth letter of the modern alphabet, the letter **m** held a different position for a time in its rather long history. It almost disappeared completely for it once was the practice to place a bar over the preceding letter instead of writing the letter, which was then omitted. It was not until the late seventeenth century that this practice began to die away. It ceased altogether about the middle of the last century.

1 First arch high: pride; egotism; condescension; poor taste.
2 Second arch high: insecure; self-conscious; needs approbation.
3 Angular: impatient; hard; humourless.
4 No middle bar: a love of freedom and the outdoors.
5 Three loops: vanity; surface social poise.
6 Three arches: compulsive; worrying nature; insecure.
7· Central loop: likes to feel in control.
8 Rounded tops: imaginative.
9 Incurved final: critical; complainer.
10 Pointed tops: little humour; inquisitive; penetrating mind.

180

11 Endstroke below base-line: stubborn; irritable; abrupt nature.
12 Like letter **u**: diet-conscious; health-faddist.
13 Modern: good judgement; straightforward.
14 Short middle stroke: ambitious; unthinking; selfish.
15 Short final stroke: lack of responsibility; lack of involvement.

A low first arch to the letter **m** will show the writer to be dependent on the feelings and opinions of others. A low second arch implies more self-sufficiency. A wide letter is indicative of extravagance and waste, but a narrow letter **m** shows inhibition and a retiring nature.

The letter n

The fourteenth letter of the present alphabet, the letter **n** has been associated and interchangeable with the letter **m**. The probable origin in the shape we use today stems from the speed with which the letter **m** was written. The letter **n** is an unfinished letter **m**.

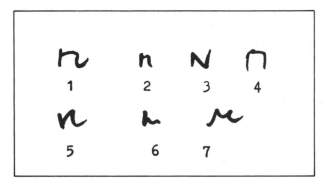

1 Wide: extravagant; wasteful.
2 Narrow: inhibited; shy.
3 Angular: capacity for detail; careful; precise.
4 Square: manual dexterity; musical or mathematical ability.
5 V formation: analytical; enquiring mind.
6 Tapering: changeable; diplomatic; sense of humour.
7 Musical note: sense of rhythm.

This letter takes on many shapes in the course of handwriting. Often, it is convenient to taper the letter. In below-average writing this letter will, if the last letter in a word or sentence, be larger than its predecessors. This shows immaturity and childishness. Intelligence may be limited.

The letter o

The letter o has a fascinating and mixed history which goes back well over three thousand years.

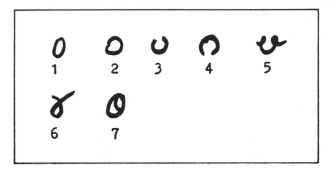

1   Narrow: inhibited; shy; secretive.
2   Wide: broadminded; tolerant.
3   Open top: talkative; moody.
4   Open base: hypocritical; untrustworthy.
5   Double loops: deceptive nature.
6   Crossed top: cold; heartless; unreliable.
7   Inner line: insincere; shrewd; clever.

The way the letter o is formed will show the amount of reliability and honesty the writer possesses. Two letter o's together should be consistent. When the difference between them is obvious, the writer will always protect his or her own interests first, and must not be taken at face value. Connecting o's which are similarly formed indicate a relatively straightforward character. There is also a certain amount of control in the overall make-up.

The letter p

The sixteenth letter of the modern alphabet, the letter **p** has survived a number of form changes as various cultures have adopted and discarded it. The current shape may be traced directly back to Roman times.

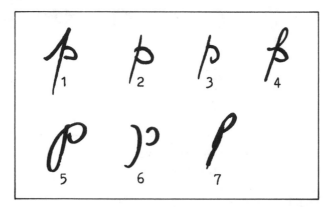

1 High angle with or without loop: argumentative.
2 Pot-lid: stubborn; wilful.
3 Open at base-line: cruel streak; dishonest; spendthrift.
4 Loop at top: emotional; sensitive; yielding nature.
5 Long loop: physically active; strength; stamina; love of outdoors.
6 In two parts: constructive; creative; manual dexterity.
7 Retraced loop: stamina; endurance.

The letter **p** is associated with outdoor and sporting activities. Two letter **p**'s together, neatly aligned and similarly executed, show the writer will pause to consider action. When different and dissimilar in height, it indicates that the writer is prone to unpredictable or inconsistent behaviour. There is a lack of physical control.

The letter q

The shape of the seventeenth letter of the alphabet has altered little through history. At one stage it was the Greek symbol for the number 90. It has been variously associated with, or used instead of, the letters c and k. The q replaced the sound for the sound of cw and kw in the Old English language. In modern English the letter u invariably follows the q.

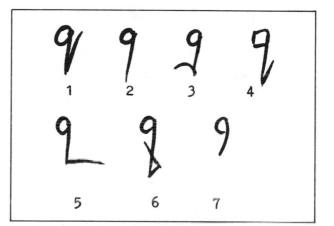

1 Long final: altruistic; kindly nature.
2 No final: vital; direct, enthusiastic.
3 Arc to left: dislikes obligations; avoids responsibilities; clannish.
4 Square: good with hands; creative; constructive.
5 Extended: vain; egotistical.
6 Triangular loop: keeps self to self; resents intrusion into privacy.
7 Musical note: musical appreciation.

An open top to the letter q reflects a tendency to criticize others without cause. If double-looped the writer will be talkative and untruthful.

The letter r

The letter r has occupied several positions in various alphabets throughout history. It is currently number eighteen, but it has been sixteen, seventeen, and twenty at various times. The present shape of the letter r owes much to Irish origins.

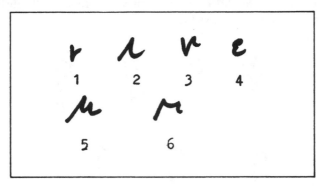

1 Plain: active; enthusiastic; swift mental approach.
2 Pointed: enquiring mind; perceptive.
3 V shape: confuses others; disconcerting.
4 Greek form: cultural interests.
5 Tall initial stroke: probing mind; critical.
6 Square: manual dexterity; constructive.

Different versions of the letter r, whether at the beginning, in the middle or at the end of words or sentences, show the degree of inconsistency present in a nature. Four or five different styles within a sample of script may be taken as normal, especially if, when checked, the differences are uniform: that is, all those at the beginning of a word are the same, and so on. Should the letter r be consistent throughout, a great deal of control is exercised by the writer.

The letter s

The letter s has held several positions and been written in different ways throughout its history. Basically, we use the Roman version today, but up to the end of the last century the letter was printed as a minuscule letter **f** which was the nearest accepted shape at the time.

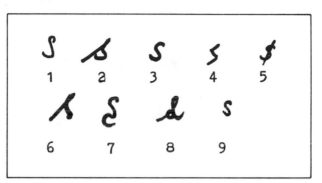

1 Tall: imaginative; taste.
2 Long initial stroke: hard; unforgiving; persevering.
3 Round: gentle; kind; yielding nature.
4 Angular: aggressive; persistent.
5 Money sign: acquisitive; collector of trivia.
6 Pointed top: sharp tongue; critical.
7 Claw base: selfish; avaricious.
8 Knotted: forcible nature; pushy.
9 Printed: rebel streak; literary mind.

In the majority of handwriting samples the letter s will appear in several shapes and styles which is quite normal. When, with very few exceptions, all the letters are executed in a similar manner, the writer is exhibiting a strong degree of control. In particular, when two letter s's are together they should be of a similar shape and form to show a fairly consistent approach. This is not always possible. As an example of this, try to write the word "possesses" several times in quick succession.

The letter t

This letter held several different positions in various alphabets throughout history before becoming established as the twentieth letter in the modern English version. In ancient times it was written like the letter c. To avoid confusion the formation was straightened and the top curve became the free-stroke bar.

1 Short bar: poor drive and enthusiasm; reserve; timidity.
2 Long bar: control; confidence; energy; ambition.
3 Heavy bar: domineering; selfish; determined.
4 Light bar: sensitive; retiring; easily influenced.
5 Ascending bar: optimistic; ambitious; enquiring mind; ardent.
6 Descending bar: depression; resignation.
7 Left of stem: cautious; indecisive.
8 Right of stem: impulse; energy; speed; quick-thinking.
9 No bar: careless; rebellious; absentminded.
10 Top bar: leadership; ambition; imagination.
11 Concave bar: self-protective; repressed emotions.
12 Convex bar: unstable; poor control; indulgent; lazy streak.

13 Wavy bar: fun-loving; sense of humour.
14 Knotted bar: tenacious; persistent; persevering.
15 Curved bar: critical nature; not always truthful.
16 Looped top of stem: talkative; vain; sensitive; emotional.
17 Stem looped: imaginative; needs approbation; lacks confidence.
18 Star shape: obstinate; logical; dislikes criticism; persistent.
19 Tent style: stubborn; dogmatic.
20 Spread stem: neurotic; lazy; suspicious.

Speed, intelligence, willpower, drive and ambition can all be detected from this letter, as can control and personal discipline. It is thought that there are more than fifty ways to cross the t.

The letter u

The twenty-first letter of the English alphabet, the letter **u** was for many years equivalent to the letter **v**. At one stage the v-shape was the capital version, while the **u**-shape was used as the minuscule. About two hundred years ago the letters were finally given their own identity.

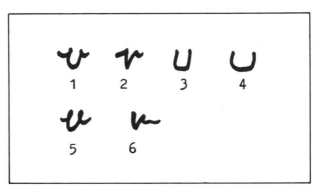

1   Garland: open; friendly; emotional.
2   Angular: determined; stubborn; awkward.
3   Square: practical; clever with hands.
4   Wide: imaginative; dramatic.
5   Looped: smooth-talking; deceptive.
6   Wavy: clever; versatile; diplomatic.

Like the letter **n**, this letter may take on many shapes. Often, it appears a little larger than the average size of the script in which it is found. This may show doubt or uncertainty, and would be emphasized in poor-quality writing. When it seems slightly smaller the writer is more confident.

The letter v

The history of the letter v is interwoven with that of the letter **u**. It was only when the **v**, as a consonant, began to be used more as an initial or capital letter that it developed a separate identity. By the start of the eighteenth century it had become the twenty-second letter of the modern English alphabet.

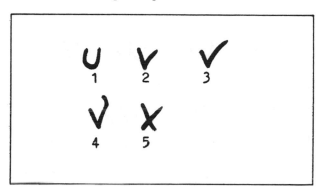

1   Rounded: open; friendly; gentle.
2   Plain: perceptive; intelligent.
3   Endstroke: enterprise; initiative; pride.
4   Returned endstroke: uncertainty; self-protection.
5   Crossed: untrustworthy.

One of the few middle-zone letters to be normally executed in the angular style, this letter often appears more rounded than one might expect. It is a good test of the depth of emotional energy.

The letter w

The letter **w** was born of the letters **u** and **v** shortly after the Norman invasion of Britain in the eleventh century. The original Saxon symbol was a double **u** written as a double **v**. The Normans disliked this practice and introduced the present symbol which is now the twenty-third letter of the modern English alphabet.

1 Angular: analytical; mentally astute; alert.
2 Centre cross: egotistical.
3 Middle loop: clever; perceptive.
4 All loops: deceptive; smooth-talker; uses people.
5 Final loop: faddish; arty; likes to be different.
6 Wavy: versatile; clever.
7 Rounded: shy; sensitive; gentle.
8 Curved final: self-protective.
9 Narrow: inhibited; retiring; narrow-minded.
10 Tall first stroke: vanity; arrogance; confidence misplaced.
11 Arcade: opportunistic; secretive.
12 Curved inward: lonely; lives on past glories.
13 Wide: broadminded; wasteful.

The letter **w** is associated with ambition and mental perception. An angular top with a rounded base shows a keen mind with an unassuming emotional nature. Mental drive is present, but there is insufficient physical presence or authority to carry through plans.

The letter x

One of the oldest letters in our alphabet, this twenty-fourth letter may well be a candidate for eventual discontinuation, since in the language of today, written or spoken, there are other letters which may be used as suitable alternatives.

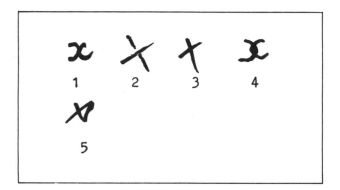

1　Two curves: chatterbox; individualist.
2　Three strokes: clever; prefers own company.
3　Below base-line: aggressive nature.
4　Linked curves: reserved; shy.
5　Looped cross: perceptive; quick; alert.

Any form of the × formation, wherever it may appear, other than as the letter **x,** shows a depressed state of mind. There may also be feelings of frustration and inadequacy.

The letter y

The letter **y** had a very mixed history until it became fully employed in its own right as the twenty-fifth letter of the modern English alphabet. It was used as a substitute for the letters **u, v, w, i** and **j**. During the Middle Ages it was used instead of the **i** by scribes, which accounts for some of the unusual spelling of certain words today.

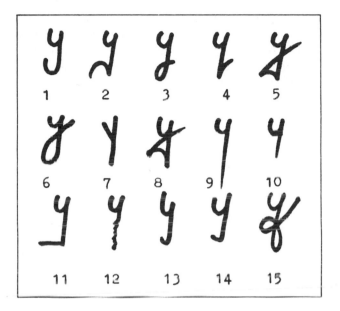

1 Open loop: restless physical nature; desire for change.
2 Arc to left: clannish; dislike of responsibility.
3 Low crossing: sexual incompatibility.
4 Like a **q**: repressed sexual drive; impotency.
5 Triangular base: cold nature; if large, domestic unrest.
6 Large loop: healthy libido; physical energy.
7 Straight lines: ability to concentrate.
8 Frog-foot: sexually incompetent; disappointment in sexual matters.
9 Long line: defensive sexually; if heavy, cruelty.
10 Short line: sublimated sex nature.

11 Left base-line: guilt in sexual matters; unrest.
12 Corkscrew: sexual aberration or deviancy.
13 High first stroke: poor leadership qualities.
14 High second stroke: good leadership potential.
15 Double loop: unusual sexual interests.

The letter **y** is acknowledged to be linked with the sexuality of the individual. Variations in lower-zone loops frequently occur, and the more they appear, the more easily stimulated the nature. Wildly varying forms may show sexual fantasy or even aberration. Note the direction of the loops: to the left, introversion; to the right, extroversion. Regular loops equal in size show a lack of sexual imagination, repression, and possible tension through sexual incompatibility.

The letter z

Once the sixth and seventh letter of ancient alphabets, the letter z was dropped altogether by some cultures. After the conquest of the Greeks, the Romans introduced it into their own language as the final letter. It is now widely used in its own right in many modern alphabets. Trends in modern orthography mean that it is used less frequently in the English alphabet.

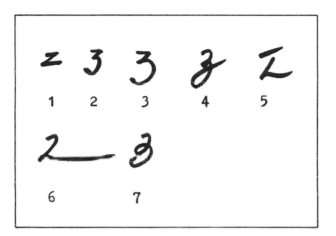

1   Printed block: direct; plain-speaking; straightforward.
2   Figure 3: materialistic.
3   Large open loop: emotional; romantic; inhibited.
4   Rounded: yielding; gentle.
5   Two parts: aspirations; ambitious; idealistic.
6   End-stroke elongated: vain.
7   Loop in centre: stubborn; determined; dogmatic.

The letter z is rarely the same twice in a sample. When radically different, it shows that the nature is inconsistent, or that control was poor at the time of writing.

Trait Index

Each character trait in a sample of handwriting is only a clue. It should never be taken in isolation as representing a feature of personality. An occasional sign may mean just that. Also remember that all aspects of personality have negative and positive facets: observe and evaluate the whole sample carefully. Bear in mind that what you have before you reflects the mood of the writer at the time of writing. Do not jump to conclusions.

ABRUPT: vertical writing; sharp endings; letters **d** and **t** ending through the base-line.

ABSENTMINDED: missing **i** dots; omitted **t** bars; gaps between letters irregular.

ACCURATE: good spacing; **i** dots and **t** bars carefully placed; small writing; good punctuation.

ACTIVE: pressure; speed; angular style; forward slant; firm downstrokes.

ADAPTABLE: round forms; garland style; even pressure; connected writing.

ADVENTUROUS: speed; broad appearance; large writing; forward slope; good spacing.

AESTHETIC: straight margins; Greek forms of letters **e**, **d** and **g**; printed capitals; good spacing and layout.

AFFECTIONATE: broad style; right-hand slant; full lower zones; garland formation.

AGGRESSIVE: heavy pressure; angular style; accent on downward strokes; narrow, sharp appearance; lower loops triangular.

ALERT: light pressure; speed; simplified style; upper zone linked from middle- or lower-zone letters.

ALTRUISTIC: forward style; speed; width in middle zone; garland formation; extended endstrokes; upper-zone emphasis.

AMBITIOUS: rising **t** bars; rising lines; large capitals; speed; lower and upper zones emphasized; uneven pressure.

ANALYTICAL: vertical style; small, but not cramped; simple forms; good spacing.

ANXIOUS: uneven style; extreme right or left slant; irregular forms; retracing; jamming together; poor spacing.

APPREHENSIVE: uneven middle zone; covering strokes; mixed slants; broken upper-zone strokes and loops.

ARDENT: wide, forward style; large writing; heavy pressure; exaggerated lower- and upper-zone loops.

ARROGANT: large capitals; flourishes in signature; angular style; heavy downward pressure; underlining.

ASSERTIVE: angular forms; heavy pressure; large signature with a full stop; firm t bar crosses; lower-zone loops triangular.

AUTHORITARIAN: high or exaggerated t bars; angular forms; unnecessary flourishes; high i dots; large capitals.

AUTOCRATIC: small text with large signature; large capitals; heavy pressure.

AVARICIOUS: abrupt endings; slow speed; vertical writing; narrow letters.

BAD MANNERED: illegible writing; illegible signature; poor general layout; jerky left margin; poor spacing.

BALANCED: regular; rhythmic; even baseline; balanced zones; even margins.

BENEVOLENT: garland forms; round style and lower-zone loops; light pressure; forward slant.

BOASTFUL: ornamentation; large capitals; large signature; artificial style; full, pasty appearance.

BROADMINDED: wide, garland forms; forward slant; short t bars; light pressure.

BRUTAL: heavy pressure; accentuated down strokes; heavy t bars; angular or arcade style; slow speed; irregularity; poor balance.

BUSINESS-MINDED: angular style; good layout; upright writing; well drawn figures; legible signature; occasional word connection.

CALM: upright style; regularity in size and zone formation; good punctuation; even pressure; average speed.

CAREFUL: closed vowel tops; even pressure and regular style; good margins; slow speed; careful i dots and t bars.

CARELESS: illegibility; poor or omitted i dots and t bars; uneven pressure; lower-zone loops mingling with upper-zone loops.

CAUTIOUS: closed vowel tops; arcade style; leftward slant; light i dots and t bars; lower-zone lead-in strokes.

CLEVER: speed; words and letters linked by t bars; lower-zone loops linked forward to middle- or upper-zone stroke of next word; good layout.

CLUMSY: upper/lower-zone loops mingling; irregular style; uneven middle zone; ornate capitals; mixed slant.

COLD: left slant; sharp writing; no loops; angular or accentuated arcades; abrupt end strokes.

COMMON-SENSIBLE: vertical style; regularity; few or no loops; straight baseline; small to medium size; good numbers.

CONCENTRATION: small size; careful i dots and t bars; good punctuation; even margins; closed vowels.

CONFIDENT: forward slope; rising base line; rising t bars; i dot dashes to the right; speed; underlined signature; simple capitals.

CONSCIENTIOUS: slow speed; upright writing; tall upper-zone loops; low i dots and t bars; even pressure; good punctuation.

CONSIDERATE: uniform height; good layout; forward slant; medium size; garland style.

CONSISTENT: balanced zones; even appearance; even spacing; even pressure; angular style; upright writing.

CONSTRUCTIVE: simplified style; printed capitals; vertical slant; even spacing and connections; even pressure; square looking.

CONVENTIONAL: forward slope; even margins; arcade style; copybook appearance; light t bars; balanced zones.

CO-OPERATIVE: forward slope; round writing; garland style; letter g like an 8; letter y like a 7; signature same size as script.

CREATIVE: original, forward style; large capitals; wide spacing of letters, words and lines; full and pasty appearance.

CRITICAL: accentuated angular style; thin writing; heavy pressure; simple forms; long or high t bars; tent shape i dots.

CRUEL: letters ending below base line; heavy pressure; thick or pasty style; narrow forms; heavy t bars; smudged i dots.

CULTURED: Greek formations; good layout; even margins; simple capitals; upright style.

CUNNING: slow speed; left slant; knots at the top of vowels; broken strokes; mixed pressure.

CURIOUS: middle-zone letters with pointed tops; high reaching upper-zone loops; high i dots and t bars.

DECEITFUL: narrow writing; closed vowels; irregular appearance; uneven pressure; exaggerated capitals or other formations; uneven baseline.

DECISIVE: upright style; firm i dots and t bars; straight down strokes; no lead in strokes; angular or definite arcade forms.

DEPENDABLE: vertical style; straight base line; balanced appearance; even margins; even pressure; moderate speed.

DETERMINED: few or no lower-zone loops; rising t bars; heavy pressure; abrupt terminals; angular style; vertical or forward slant.

DIPLOMATIC: upright style; closed vowels; simple form; arcade with thread connections; middle-zone letters decreasing in size.

DIRECT: even appearance; good margins; simplified capital and t bars; no starting strokes; abrupt terminals.

DISCERNING: wide spacing between words and lines; points on middle-zone letters and at tips of upper- and lower-zone loops.

DISHONEST: irregular slant; uneven appearance; breaks in base of middle-zone letters; counter-strokes; double-walling or knotting of vowels; blotchiness; exaggerations; illegibility.

DISORGANIZED: mingling lines; uneven spacing; poor margins; variable slant; omitted or irregular i dots and t bars.

DISSOLUTE: shaky appearance; poor form and layout; pasty or blotchy; concave t bars; long, full, badly made lower-zone loops.

DOGMATIC: sharp pressure; rising lines; heavy t bars; angular or arcade style; abrupt terminals.

DOMINEERING: heavy t bars and roofing capitals; heavy pressure; vertical style; large, underlined signature with a full stop.

DRAMATIC: garland style; upper and lower zones accentuated; inflated upper loops; triangular lower loops.

DREAMY: exaggerated upper loops; forward slant; ornamentation; high i dots and t bars; disconnected writing.

DULL: copybook style; upright or slightly forward slant; connected forms; regularity; lean writing.

DYNAMIC: large, rightward slant; full lower zone; angular style; heavy pressure; signature larger than script and underlined.

EASILY INFLUENCED: broad, garland forms; copybook style; round appearance.

EASY-GOING: regular, garland style; light pressure; upper- and lower-zone loops rounded.

ECCENTRIC: illegibility, wild formations; artificial enrollments;

unusual punctuation, ink or paper colours; illegible signature.

EDUCATED: Greek formations; good spacing and general layout; upright or slight variation either way; speed; good connections; decrease in size of words or letters.

EFFICIENT: few or no loops; speed; arcade style; upright formation; good spacing.

EGOTISTICAL: over-large capitals; letters very wide; over-fussy upper- and lower-zone loops; heavy pressure; unusual or illegible signature.

EMOTIONAL: copybook, or round writing; right-hand slant; over-sized loops in upper and lower zones; full middle zone; irregular appearance.

ENDURING: good, even pressure; regular style; upright writing; angular.

ENERGETIC: heavy pressure; angular or arcade style; firm down strokes; speed; i dots and t bars well to the right; long lower-zone loops.

ENTERPRISING: potlids; normal middle zone but oversized upper and lower zones; heavy pressure; rightward slant.

EROTIC: full, leftward-tending lower-zone loops; strong pressure; pasty appearance.

EXCITABLE: rising base line; irregular appearance; starting strokes; rightward slope; high dash-like i dots; some threading.

EXTRAVAGANT: increasing margins; wide spacing; extended terminals; fullness in upper and lower zones; large script.

EXTROVERT: large capitals and personal pronoun; fast speed; rightward slant; oversize writing.

FAITHFUL: well formed letters; even base line; vertical style; natural punctuation; legible signature.

FASHIONABLE: pasty; full middle zone; unusual ink and paper colours; circle i dots; upright writing.

FASTIDIOUS: slow speed; attention to detail; good punctuation; upright writing; small and legible; light pressure.

FATIGUED: weak or shaky writing; descending lines; light pressure.

FLIRTATIOUS: rising base line; extended or curling endstrokes; pasty forward slant; poor lower-zone loops.

FORGETFUL: irregular spaces between letters and words;

omitted letters, words, i dots and t bars; disconnected writing.

FORMAL: upright style; initials used with surname in signature; arcade formation; wide upper-zone loops.

FRANK: wide script; strong pressure; garland style; even baseline.

FRIENDLY: garland style; rightward slant; open-topped vowels; extended terminals.

FRUSTRATED: upright or leftward slope; knotted tops to middle-zone vowels; points on upper- and lower-zone loops; signature crossed through or encircled.

FUNLOVING: wavy t bars; fast speed; rightward slant; wide upper- and lower-zone loops; irregular base line; broad and pasty.

FUSSY: accurate punctuation, i dots and t bars; small, vertical style; even zones.

GENEROUS: rightward slant; wide margins; long lower-zone loops; heavy pressure; garland style.

GENTLE: light pressure; garland style; round appearance; rounded tops and bottoms to middle-zone letters.

GENUINE: legible; vertical slant; signature same as script.

GOSSIPY: open middle-zone vowels at the top; poor spacing; rightward slant.

GREEDY: poor numerals; poor formation and layout; narrow margins; hooks on terminals and lower-zone strokes instead of loops.

GREGARIOUS: narrow gaps between words; rightward slant; extended horizontal terminal strokes.

HASTY: narrow right-hand margin; quick speed; right-hand slant; high-flying i dots and t bars well to the right.

HELPFUL: broad middle zone; rightward slant; extended terminal strokes; garland style.

HIGHLY STRUNG: mixed slant; irregular base line; poor layout; larger-than-average size; shaky pressure; points to loops.

HIGH-SPIRITED: open-topped vowels; rising base lines; all three zones full; rightward slant; garland formation.

HONEST: right slant; middle-zone vowels closed at the top; even base line; legible with legible signature; speed; no embellishments.

HUMOROUS: garland connections; wavy t bars; broad and pasty writing.

HYPOCHONDRIAC: retraced letters; narrow writing; leftward slant; threading.

HYPOCRITICAL: arcade style; illegibility; slow speed; middle-zone letters open at baseline; uneven pressure.

IDEALISTIC: predominant upper zone; rising end strokes and base lines; weak pressure; poor lower-zone formations.

IMAGINATIVE: upper-zone emphasis; high placed t bars; full and broad writing; plenty of loops in both upper and lower zones.

IMMATURE: rounded tops and bottoms to middle-zone letters; large, copybook script; poor upper-zone loops; poor layout.

IMPATIENT: speed; rightward slant; weak pressure; i dots and t bars to the right; poor punctuation; neglected style.

IMPULSIVE: irregular rightward slant; poor punctuation; disconnected letters; rising base line.

INCONSIDERATE: illegibility; poor layout; dominant middle zone; wide or uneven left margin; illegible signature.

INCONSISTENT: mixed slant; uneven left margin; capital letters in wrong places; variable size in middle zone; uneven pressure.

INDEPENDENT: wide spacing between letters, words and lines; vertical writing; even baseline; printed or separated capital from rest of word.

INDIVIDUAL: speed; originality; vertical style; even pressure; signature and text similar size; good spacing; tasteful ornamentation.

INEFFICIENT: variation in slant; mingling lower and upper zones; poor line and word spacing; irregular base line; slow speed.

INHIBITED: leftward slant; few or no loops in lower zone; arcade style; cover strokes; slow speed; closed middle-zone vowels.

INITIATIVE, SHOWING: rightward slant; disconnected script; high-flying i dots and t bars; speed; average pressure; rising base line.

INSECURE: mixed slant; small i in comparison to middle-zone size; narrow spacing; variable pressure.

INTELLIGENCE: words diminishing in size; speed; rising base line; upright writing; good layout and spacing; pointed tops to middle-zone letters.

INTENSE: controlled base line; heavy pressure on down-strokes;

small angular style; connected formation.

INTOLERANT: leftward slant; narrow, cramped style; letters ending below base line; potlids; full stop after signature.

INTROVERT: leftward slant; arcade style; knotted vowels; up and down emphasis.

INTUITIVE: disconnected writing; some threading; needle-point tops and bottoms of middle-zone letters; long extensions in upper and lower zones.

INVENTIVE: good spacing; original script; legible and quick speed.

IRRESPONSIBLE: irregular base line; mixed slant; weak t bars; poor punctuation.

IRRITABLE: variable heavy pressure; ticks or hooks; pointed ends to loops; angular script; letters extending below baseline.

JEALOUS: narrow, leftward slant; varying pressure; hooks and ticks on lower- and upper-zone starting strokes; large middle-zone vowels.

KIND: right slant; large writing; extended end strokes; garland formations; some disconnections.

LAZY: rounded middle zone; slow speed; irregular spacing; short descenders; weak pressure; uneven base line.

LEADERSHIP-PRONE: large writing; steady pressure; rightward slant; good layout.

LEVELHEADED: vertical script; even base line; firm pressure.

LONELY: narrow spacing; narrow margins; large middle zone; descending base line.

LOYAL: good base line; vertical script; good connections; arcade style; legible signature and script.

LUCID: balanced margins; even base lines; even spacing between lines and words; simple style; legibility.

MATERIALISTIC: heavy lower-zone emphasis; pasty writing; thick pressure; claws instead of loops; left or vertical slant.

MATURE: good spacing and layout; vertical writing; speed; originality; good punctuation.

MEAN: small or no margins; small script; no endstrokes; hooks and ticks; words close together.

MODEST: small writing; small plain capitals; light pressure; well placed i dots and t bars; signature smaller than script.

MOODY: irregular base line; mixed slant; uneven pressure.

NAIVE: garland style; i open middle-zone vowels; copybook formation.

NARROWMINDED: arcade style; narrow cramped formation; middle-zone emphasis; thin writing.

NATURAL: garland style; speed; simple formations; undulating baseline.

NEAT: even margins; small vertical writing; even punctuation; original style; precise t bars.

NERVOUS: pressure changes; uneven baseline; mixed slant; poor punctuation; shaky strokes; points on end of loops.

NOSY: right slant; open top vowels; poor margins, unnecessary strokes; vulgar capitals; poor numeracy.

OBJECTIVE: small precise writing; vertical slant; regular baseline; even pressure; some disconnections.

OBSERVANT: precise punctuation; disconnected writing; disconnected capitals which may be printed; small script; small signature.

OBSESSIVE: very narrow or very wide script; hooks and ticks; artificial base line; broken loops; uneven gaps; angular or arcade style.

OBSTINATE: full stop after signature; potlids; lower loops triangular; heavy up-and-down pressure; hooks and heavy t bars.

OBSTRUCTIVE: lower-zone loops reversed; leftward slant; heavy pressure downward; enriched starting strokes.

OPEN-MINDED: vertical slant; garland or threading script; open top middle-zone vowels; even spacing.

OPPORTUNISTIC: forward slope; speed; lower-zone to upper-zone linking; thread connections.

OPTIMISTIC: wide right slant; rising base line; high-flying i dots and t bars well to the right; garland formation.

ORGANIZED: vertical slant; small script; accurate punctuation; good layout; even baseline; legibility.

ORIGINAL: good spacing; tasteful ornamentation as opposed to copybook; flowing, artistic and legible.

OSTENTATIOUS: excessive ornamentation; large capitals; full pasty style; ornate or illegible signature; unusual paraphs.

PASSIONATE: heavy pressure; pasty; right slope; full upper and lower zones; rounded style with some angular signs.

PATIENT: slow speed; precise punctuation; small script, even margins.

PATRONIZING: t bars covering words; high first arch on letter m; high, or ornate capitals; underlined signature.

PEDANTIC: thread connections; accurate punctuation; steady baseline.

PERCEPTIVE: disconnected letters and capitals; small script; wide spacing of letters, words and lines; pointed loops in upper zone.

PERSISTENT: knotted t bars; steady base line; hooks and ticks on starting strokes; angular or arcade style; even pressure.

PESSIMISTIC: light i dots and t bars; weak punctuation; falling baselines; arcade style; uneven middle zone.

POISED: vertical slant; arcade or angular formation; even baselines; good margins and layout; printed capitals.

POMPOUS: large writing; enriched signature; high capitals; full middle zone.

POSSESSIVE: large script, signature and capitals; hooks and ticks; middle-zone emphasis; leftward slant; heavy pressure.

PRACTICAL: lower-zone emphasis; square appearance; vertical slant; thin pressure; even baselines.

PREJUDICED: mixed or extreme slant; potlids; letters descending below baseline.

PROCRASTINATING: low i dots and t bars to the left; slow speed; starting strokes; poor layout.

PROGRESSIVE: wide right slant; rising baselines; speed; high-flying i dots and t bars.

PROMISCUOUS: variable pressure; heavy lower-zone emphasis; mingling lines; arcade style.

PROTECTIVE: extended terminals; full middle zone; roofing strokes; right slant.

PUNCTUAL: good spacing; accurate punctuation; legibility; even baseline.

QUARRELSOME: lower-zone loops triangular; dash i dots; low starting strokes; arcade or angular style; letters ending below base line; full stop and underlining of signature.

QUIET: light pressure; garland style; leftward slant; small

writing; even base line.

RASH: forward slant; widening left margin; high-flying i dots; poor punctuation; speed; cramped right-hand margin.

RATIONAL: upright style; small writing; even margins; few or no loops in upper zone.

REALISTIC: regular, small script; vertical slant; middle-zone emphasis.

REBELLIOUS/REBEL STREAK: reverse loops; poor punctuation; leftward slant.

RECEPTIVE: light pressure; garland style; connected writing; irregular script.

RELIABLE: regular, vertical script; firm base lines; even margins; good layout; balanced zones; legibility.

RESERVED: leftward slope; arcade or angular script; closed letters; small capitals.

RESPECTFUL: low i dots and t bars; garland style; ascending arch on letters m and w; even margins; copybook script.

RESPONSIBLE: balanced zones; even margins; vertical slant; even pressure.

RESTLESS: uneven baseline; mingling lines; poor layout; irregular zone emphasis; disconnected writing.

ROMANTIC: garland style; right slant; long or full upper- and lower-zone loops.

RUDE: poor margins and layout; illegibility; signature unreadable and underscored; mixed slant; poor numerals.

RUTHLESS: tight, narrow writing; few or no loops; angular style; heavy pressure; signature underscored and with full stop.

SAD: falling baseline; weak pressure; thin writing.

SARCASTIC: angular style; potlids; heavy downstrokes; strong t bars; sharp writing.

SCEPTICAL: arcade or angular style; vertical slant; connected letters.

SECRETIVE: arcade style; leftward slant; covering strokes; terminals turning back.

SELF-CONSCIOUS: small, left slant; narrow writing; garland style; margins even; baseline unnaturally steady.

SELF-DISCIPLINED: vertical slant; arcade or angular style; even pressure; baseline steady; good layout.

SELFISH: left slant; middle-zone emphasis; large writing; uneven pressure; heavy paraphs with full stop under signature.

SENSIBLE: balanced zones; upright writing; good layout; consistent punctuation; straight baseline; connected writing.

SENSITIVE: uneven pressure; loops in letters **d** and **t**; extreme left or right slant; mixed slant; irregular baseline.

SENTIMENTAL: garland style; right-hand slant; accentuated loops in lower and upper zone; large writing.

SEXY: full lower zone; medium-heavy pressure; mingling lines; garland style if overt; arcade style if secretive; few or no loops if mental approach preferred; enrolled or ornamented capitals and strokes.

SHALLOW: emphasis on middle zone; arcade style; uneven base line; unusual paraphs with signature.

SHREWD: middle-zone emphasis; vertical or leftward slant; poor terminals.

SHY: wide writing; uneven baseline; small script and signature; wide margin to the right.

SINCERE: speed; even baseline; signature matches script; no underlining; legibility; good punctuation.

SLY: mixed slant; uneven base line; poor punctuation; wide garland style; threadiness.

SNOBBISH: large capitals; covering strokes; over-large personal pronoun; arcade or angular formation; excessively neat.

SOCIABLE: right slant; connected style; garland formation; open middle-zone vowels at the top.

SPITEFUL: sharp, angular writing; ends of loops pointed in upper and lower zone; slow speed.

STABLE: clear punctuation; vertical slant; good spacing; even baseline.

STUBBORN: reversed loops in lower zone; letters descending below base line; full stop after signature.

SUBJECTIVE: large, full writing; large signature; open or wide writing.

SUPERIOR: signature larger than script; underlining; arcade style; descending arches in letter **m**; **t** bars at top of stem.

SYSTEMATIC: even margins; steady baseline; small writing; vertical style; angular formation.

TACTFUL: thread connections; middle-zone threading; single stroke on personal pronoun.

TACTLESS: right slant; middle-zone vowel tops left open; garland style; illegibility; uneven baseline; copybook formation.

TALKATIVE: middle-zone letters open at top; uneven pressure; poor margins and layout; garland style.

TEMPERAMENTAL: unsteady baseline; mixed slant in same words; variable pressure; mingling lines.

TENACIOUS: angular and arcade writing; leftward or upright slant; heavy pressure; letters descending below baseline; hooks and ticks.

TENSE: variable pressure; shaky writing; unsteady base line; mixed styles and slants.

THRIFTY: leftward slant; narrow margins; small writing; shortened terminals.

TIDY: vertical writing; good punctuation; steady base line; good layout; angular or arcade style.

TIMID: weak pressure; descending base line; garland style; small letter i in comparison; low capitals.

TOLERANT: garland style; right slant; round tops and bottoms in middle zone; light t bars.

TRENDY: right slant; quick speed; unusual ink or paper colour; circle i dots; wide upper- and lower-zone loops.

TRUSTWORTHY: vertical or right slant; steady base line; good punctuation; garland style; terminals extended; balanced zones.

TRUTHFUL: speed; no covering strokes; steady base line; closed vowel tops; right slant; signature matches script.

UNCONVENTIONAL: circle i dots; use of coloured paper and inks; wavering baseline; middle-zone emphasis; mixed slant.

UNCO-OPERATIVE: leftward slant; full stop after signature; angular or arcade style; potlids; hooks and ticks.

UNFAITHFUL: mixed slant; variable pressure; unsteady baseline; thread and garland style; variable middle zone.

UNPREDICTABLE: thread connections; circle i dots; missing punctuation; unsteady baseline; letters or words omitted.

UNRECEPTIVE: angular style; leftward slant; hooks and ticks; thready terminals; reversed loops.

UNRELIABLE: illegible script and signature; concave base line;

variable pressure; mixed slant.

UNSELFISH: right slant; legibility; wide spaces; steady base line; small script and signature.

UNSETTLED: disconnected writing; mixed slant; garland style; wavy base line.

UNTIDY: uneven base line; mixed slant; poor layout and margin allowance; mingling lines; variable letter and word spacing.

VAIN: large capitals; large signature; unusual paraphs; inflated loops in both upper and lower zones.

VENGEFUL: pointed loops in lower and upper zones; angular style; heavy pressure; sharp t bars; extreme or mixed slant.

VERSATILE: good balance between zones; mixed styles; disconnected script.

VITAL: speed; rising base line; heavy pressure; right slant; high-flying i dots and t bars.

VIVACIOUS: tall capitals; speed; broad writing; right slant; rising base line; high i dots and t bars.

VULGAR: artificial style; pasty; heavy pressure; ornate capitals; poor spacing; illegibility; ornamental signature.

WARMHEARTED: garland style; right slant; broad writing; full lower-zone loops; some disconnectedness.

WEAKWILLED: mixed slant; irregular baseline; poor punctuation; low pressure; short t bars and stems; letter i small by comparison.

WILLPOWER, STRONG IN: firm pressure; good spacing; connected writing; arcade style; correctly placed i dots and t bars; vertical slant.

WITTY: stepped words and lines; open tops to vowels; wavy t bars; i dots curved; some disconnected writing; any style.

WORRY-PRONE: narrow spacing; falling baseline; upper- and lower-zone loops with points; retouched letters.

YIELDING: weak pressure; small letter i; t bars low and short; small writing; extreme right or left slant; round tops to middle-zone letters; undersized capitals; small signature.

ZEALOUS: right slant; high-flying i dots and t bars; speed; heavy pressure; rising baseline; middle-zone emphasis.

Glossary

ANGULAR WRITING: Script which appears more full of angles than curves.

ARCADE WRITING: Script which seems composed of many round arches which may resemble a series of the letter **m**.

ASCENDER: Any stroke or line into the upper zone.

BASE LINE: The (imaginary) horizontal line which is formed by the bases of middle-zone letters.

BLOCK CAPITAL: Printed upper-case letters.

BODY OF SCRIPT: Usually the middle-zone area; that which is occupied by the small letters.

BROAD WRITING: Wide shaped horizontal writing.

CONCAVE SCRIPT: Writing which begins on the base line, sinks below, then rises again to the base line.

CONNECTEDNESS: An old graphological term for any form of letter or word connection by line, stroke or other means.

CONTRACTION: Letters or words which seem decreased in size in relation to the main body of script.

CONVEX SCRIPT: Writing which begins on the base line, rises upward, then sinks again to the base line.

COPYBOOK: The basic style of script as taught in school. This may vary slightly in the United Kingdom from area to area. Each country has its own system.

COUNTERSTROKE: A mark which may distort the accepted formation of a letter.

COVERSTROKE: Upward or downward extensions which are covered on return, thus narrowing an (intended) loop.

CURLICUE: A decorative curl or twist to the normal standard letter formation.

DESCENDER: Any stroke or line into the lower zone.

DIACRITIC: A sign used to indicate different sounds or values of letters. Collective term for **i** dots and **t** crosses. (Sometimes, mistakenly, used in reference to punctuation.)

DISCONNECTEDNESS: Writing in which letters or words are not continuously joined together.

DOUBLEWALLED: Term for a double effect of the middle zone of the letters **a, d, g, o** and **p.**

EMBELLISHMENT: Enriched or unnecessary additions to the normal standard of letter formations.

FORM LEVEL: The general standard of appearance of a body of script.

FULLNESS: Emphasized style and width of letters and words.

GARLAND WRITING: Handwriting which seems composed of many waves like a series of the letter **w.** Round writing style.

GRAPHIC: Written descriptive matter.

GREEK FORM: The special formation of certain letters in the Greek style, especially the letters **d, e** and **g.**

HALF OVAL: A feature which may occur in the letter **m** or **n** when the down stroke curves to the left in slow handwriting.

HOOK: An introductory or final mark which may be either as a forward or backward stroke. Sometimes called a claw.

HORIZONTAL ZONES: The area for assessing handwriting which takes into account the fact that letters may be broad, medium or narrow, thus expanding or contracting the script.

LAYOUT: The arrangement of the writing on the page.

LEAN WRITING: A script which appears thin but not spidery.

LOOPS: Strokes that curve in loops over themselves. Loops may appear in all three zones and are always indicative of emotion.

LOWER ZONE: The area below the base line which applies to the letters **g, j, p, q, y,** and **z.**

MIDDLE ZONE: The space occupied by the letters **a, c, e, m, n, o, r, s, u, v, w** and **x.**

MINGLING: Where lower-zone descenders mix with the upper zone ascenders of the line below.

NARROW WRITING: Script which appears squeezed or constricted.

NEGLECTED SCRIPT: Simplified writing which may omit certain accepted strokes but which still remains recognizable.

OVALS: Letters, or parts of letters, in the middle zone which are normally round in shape.

PARAPH: A mark or flourish made after a signature.

PASTY: Thick pressure which is accentuated with the use of a felt tip or fountain pen. Also known as pastose.

POSTPLACED: The positioning of **i** dots and **t** bars to the right of the stem.

POTLIDS: The extra length to an upper- or lower-zone stroke which makes the letter resemble a pot with a wide lid on its side.

PREPLACED: The positioning of **i** dots and **t** bars to the left of the stem.

PRESSURE: The quality of impression of a stroke, which may range from very heavy to very light, horizontally or vertically.

PUNCTUATION: Recognized stops and marks used in writing.

REGULARITY: Uniformity of appearance, stroke or pressure.

RESTING POINT: A mark produced by a pen when it is allowed to pause during the act of writing.

RETROGRESSIVE: Any motion or stroke to the left of a page.

RHYTHMIC WRITING: Fluent or naturally flowing script which is harmonious in appearance.

ROOFING: A flourish or extended bar over a body of script. The capital **T** is often used to roof over a line of writing.

SCRIPT: A sample of handwriting.

SIGNATURE: A person's name, initial or mark used as identification in signing.

SIZE RATIO: The relative proportions of long, medium or narrow letters. The accepted size of the middle zone is 3mm, with an allowance of a further 3mm each for the upper- and lower-zone extensions.

SLANT: Also known as slope. Handwriting may slant rightward, be vertical or appear reclined to the baseline. Frequently there will be a variety of slants within one sample.

SPACING: The distance between letters, words and lines.

SPEED: Whether writing is fast or slow can be judged by certain distinctive factors within the script.

STEM: The upright stroke of letters such as the **d**, **i** or **t**.

STEPPED LINE: A line in which each separate word is found to be slanting. The beginning of each word is on the base line while the end may rise or fall.

STROKE: An additional mark to the basic letter formation. It can be at the beginning or end of a letter or word. It may be in the form of a claw, hook, knot, potlid or tick. It can be firm or broken.

THREAD: A form of handwriting in which the formation tapers

in the middle or at the end of a word.

TRIANGLE: An angular formation of a loop.

UPPER ZONE: The area of handwriting above the middle of the body of script which applies to the letters **b, d, f, h, k, l** and **t**.

UPRIGHT: Any script which does not incline or recline more than five degrees away from the vertical.

ZONES:The three areas for assessing how letters have been formed: upper, middle and lower. Each zone represents a specific area of human experience. Zone balance shows maturity and control.

Select Bibliography

Jacoby, H.J., *Self-Knowledge through Handwriting* (Dent, London, 1941).

Olyanova, N., *Handwriting Tells* (Wilshire, Hollywood, 1969).

Ranald, J., *Pens and Personalities* (Vision Press, London, 1959).

Roman, K., *Handwriting, a Key to Personality* (Pantheon, New York, 1952).

Saudek, R., *Psychology of Handwriting* (Allen & Unwin, London, 1925).

Schooling, J.H., *Handwriting and Expression* (Kegan Paul, London, 1892).

Singer, E., *Manual of Graphology* (Duckworth, London, 1959).

West, P., *Graphology, Understanding What Handwriting Reveals* (Aquarian Press, London, 1981).

Index

219

culture, sense of, 201
cunning, 201
curiosity, 170, 201
curlicues, 129
cursive writing, 11, 115
curved style, 69

deceit, 65, 72, 94, 166, 167, 171, 183, 190, 192, 201–2
decisiveness, 96, 202
defiance, 19, 83
defensiveness, 19, 34, 83, 65, 97, 100, 101, 117, 130, 170
dependability, 202
depression, 88, 121, 188, 194
descenders, 34, 213
despondency, 24
detachment, 112
detail, 25, 62, 88, 89, 92, 94, 96, 103, 149, 160, 175, 182
determination, 34, 70, 76, 128, 168, 172, 174, 178, 188, 190, 197, 202
diplomacy, 99, 182, 190, 202
directness, 149, 177, 185, 197, 202
discernment, 177, 202
discipline, 37, 42, 101, 132, 189
disconnectedness, 64, 213
discrimination, 134
dishonesty, 165, 166, 167, 184, 202
disorganization, 202
dissolution, 202
distortion, 53
dogmatism, 197, 202
domestic relations, 131–5
dominance, 70, 202
doodles, 145–64
drama, sense of, 202
dreaminess, 33, 106, 149, 166, 170, 174, 179, 202
drive, 99, 143, 189
dullness, 202
dynamism, 202

easygoingness, 202
eccentricity, 175, 202
economy, 81, 84
education, 79, 203
effeminacy, 112, 178
efficiency, 93, 178, 203
ego, 31, 43, 50, 152, 154, 156, 158, 167, 168, 172, 180, 185, 192, 203
embellishments, 95, 125–30, 214; on numbers, 102–4
emotion, 12, 20, 28–9, 48, 51, 58, 76, 77, 119, 140, 150, 155, 169, 174, 178, 179, 184, 189, 190, 191, 197, 203
emphasis, 41
endings, 8, 9, 25
end strokes. See final strokes
endurance, 184, 203
energy, 39, 40, 61, 76, 143, 170, 171, 172–3, 177, 188, 195, 203
enterprise, 168, 191, 203
entertainers, 51, 75
enthusiasm, 23, 61, 63, 80, 87, 126, 175, 185, 186

envelopes, addressing, 9, 105–10
environment, 27, 79, 132
eroticism, 203
exaggeration, 56
excitability, 203
excitement, 112
expansiveness, 43, 113
extravagance, 36, 79, 181, 182, 192, 203
extroversion, 12, 14, 36, 45, 87, 132, 134, 175, 196, 203

faddishness, 175, 181, 192
faithfulness, 203
fantasizing, 106, 196
fashion, 203
fastidiousness, 113, 203
fatalism, 171
fatigue, 203
final strokes, 98–102
flexibility, 21, 25, 76
flirtatiousness, 203
flourishes, 9, 104, 125–30
forcefulness, 39
forenames, 123–6, 127
forensic analysis, 9
forgery, 9, 99, 115
forgetfulness, 203–4
form level, 9, 91, 214
formality, 70, 77, 125, 171, 178, 204
forward-sloping writing. See inclined writing
frankness, 204
freedom, 180
friendliness, 50, 70, 73, 79, 94, 101, 110, 124, 157, 162, 170, 190, 191, 204
frivolity, 74
frustration, 59, 151, 194, 204
full stops, 88, 89, 121
fun, sense of, 80, 169, 171, 175, 189, 204
fussiness, 93, 96, 113, 167, 204
future, 80, 82, 98, 112

garland writing, 69–70, 72, 73–4, 98, 101, 162, 214
generosity, 46, 79, 93, 166, 170, 204
gentleness, 191, 192, 197, 204
genuineness, 204
gossip, 204
graphology, 7, 9
graphomania, 115
greed, 57, 204
gregariousness, 14, 47, 204

hardness, 174, 180, 187
harmony, 49
haste, 204
health, 52, 57
helpfulness, 204
hesitancy, 34, 97
high-spiritedness, 204
homosexuality, 61
honesty, 102, 143, 149, 165, 183, 204
hooks, 101, 214
horizontal zones, 27, 35–7
humility, 117